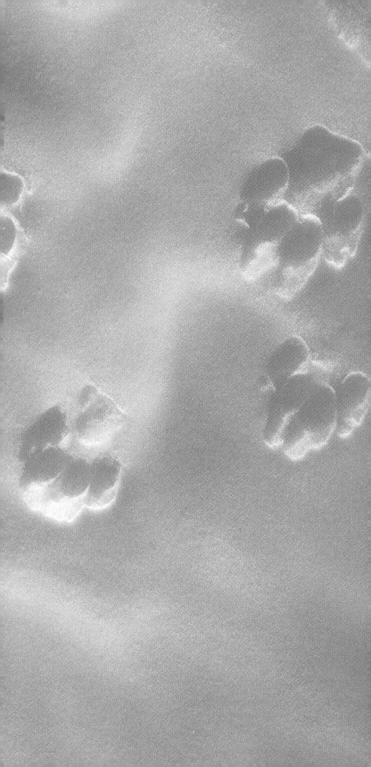

ALASKA'S
MAMMALS

A GUIDE TO SELECTED SPECIES

TEXT BY DAVE SMITH · PHOTOGRAPHS BY TOM WALKER

ALASKA NORTHWEST BOOKS™
Anchorage • Seattle • Portland

Acknowledgments

I'd like to thank the following people for reviewing the manuscript: Alaska Department of Fish and Game biologists Kathy Frost (marine mammals) and Howard Golden (furbearers); Gerald Garner, U.S. Fish and Wildlife Service (polar bears and arctic animals); Dr. Ed West, Alaska Natural Heritage Program (University of Alaska Anchorage). Tom Walker's advice and encouragement are much appreciated. I'm grateful to Ann Chandonnet of Alaska Northwest Books for starting this project and to managing editor Ellen Wheat, who had the patience to see me through it plus a sly sense of humor that made it fun. Most of all, I thank my wife, Donna, who tolerates my wild ways.

—D.S.

Second printing 1998

Library of Congress Cataloging-in-Publication Data
Smith, Dave, 1950–
  Alaska's mammals : a guide to selected species / text by Dave Smith;
photographs by Tom Walker.
    p.   cm. — (Alaska pocket guide)
  Includes bibliographical references (p. 92) and index.
  ISBN 0-88240-463-6 (acid-free paper)
    1. Mammals—Alaska.   2. Mammals—Alaska—Pictorial works.
  I. Walker, Tom, 1945–   II. Title.   III. Series.
QL719.A55S54   1995
599'.09798—dc20   95-4986
                                                                      CIP

Managing Editor: Ellen Harkins Wheat
Editor: Don Graydon
Production Editor: Kris Fulsaas
Designer: Elizabeth Watson
Map: Vikki Leib

All photos are by Tom Walker except the following: p. 54, *Wolverine*, Daniel J. Cox; p. 58, *Beluga whale*, Kathy Frost; p. 60, *Bowhead whale*, John Craighead George; p. 64, *Gray whale*, Mark McDermott; and p. 76, *Ringed seal*, Brendan P. Kelly.

PHOTOS: Front cover: *Lynx, Denali National Park and Preserve.* End papers: *Tracks of two gray wolves, Denali National Park and Preserve.* Title page: *Sea otter.* Back cover: *Polar Bear.*

Alaska Northwest Books™
An imprint of Graphic Arts Center Publishing Company
P.O. Box 10306, Portland, OR 97296-0306
800-452-3032

CONTENTS

Discovering Alaska's Mammals 7

11 LAND MAMMALS

12 Arctic Fox
14 Arctic Ground Squirrel
16 Beaver
18 Black Bear
20 Brown/Grizzly Bear
22 Caribou
24 Dall Sheep
26 Hoary Marmot
28 Lynx
30 Marten
32 Moose
34 Mountain Goat
36 Musk Ox
38 Pika
40 Porcupine
42 Red Fox
44 River Otter
46 Short-tailed Weasel
48 Sitka Black-tailed Deer
50 Snowshoe Hare
52 Wolf
54 Wolverine

57 MARINE MAMMALS

58 Beluga Whale
60 Bowhead Whale
62 Dall Porpoise
64 Gray Whale
66 Harbor Seal
68 Humpback Whale
70 Killer Whale
72 Northern Fur Seal
74 Polar Bear
76 Ringed Seal
78 Sea Otter
80 Steller Sea Lion
82 Walrus

Where to View Alaska's Mammals 85
Map of Alaska 87
Suggested Reading 92
Index 93

Bull musk ox forages on grasses in the sand dunes of Nunivak Island.

Discovering Alaska's Mammals

A prime lure of Alaska is its extraordinary wealth of wildlife. Alaska is home to herds of caribou that number in the hundreds of thousands. There are more brown/grizzly bears just on Admiralty Island than in the entire Lower 48 states. Whales by the thousands summer in Alaskan waters. But it's not only the sheer number of animals that draws people to America's last frontier. It's also the appeal of compelling creatures such as gray wolves and sea otters and the presence of polar bears, musk oxen, and other wildlife that are found only in the Far North.

This book provides an intimate glimpse of 35 of Alaska's best known land and sea mammals. For each mammal, you'll find a photo, along with a brief essay that focuses on the animal's special behaviors and on adaptations it has made to survive in the cold North. A fact box for each animal gives information on size, color, reproduction, life span, food, predators, habitat, and range. Whether you're a biologist from Fairbanks or a visitor from Florida, you'll find something of unusual interest in the discussion on each of the mammals.

Each animal chosen for this book fits into one or more of five categories: mammals native to Alaska that are not found elsewhere in the United States, such as walrus and Dall sheep; mammals that clearly hold a special interest for many people, such as gray wolves and humpback whales; pairs of mammals that have a close predator-prey relationship, such as the lynx and snowshoe hare; mammals that are similar to relatives far to the south but that have adapted to Alaska's severe climate, such as the arctic fox; and animals that by virtue of their size, habits, or habitat fill out a representative picture of Alaskan mammals.

Some of Alaska's mammals live in an environment that's as barren as the moon, and just as foreign to most people. Ice is the critical element. When winter arrives, the Arctic Ocean and Chukchi Sea freeze from the North Pole south toward Alaska. Eventually ice chokes the Bering Strait between Alaska and Russia, then moves down into the Bering Sea to a point more than 200 miles south of St. Lawrence Island.

The advancing ice brings polar bears that have been living for the summer on the permanent pack ice surrounding the

North Pole. Female walrus and their young move along the southern edge of the ice all year. Gray whales stay ahead of the ice as it moves south, then continue on a migratory route that takes them to Mexico.

With the arrival of spring, the ice recedes from Alaska back toward the North Pole and thousands of animals advance northward. When the waters of the Bering Strait and beyond are again clear of ice, millions of birds and mammals return to the incredibly food-rich waters of the Chukchi Sea and the Arctic Ocean as well as to all of Alaska's coastal waters, where long daylight hours trigger growth of microscopic plants and animals at the bottom of the food chain.

Spring's arrival triggers movement among Alaska's land mammals, too. Caribou in the 180,000-strong Porcupine herd begin a 300-mile northward migration toward the coastal plains of the Arctic National Wildlife Refuge. As snow melts in the high country and plants begin to grow, moose start moving up into the mountains. Bears and marmots emerge from their dens after a long winter sleep.

Getting a personal look at these mammals in their own territory can be an exciting and inspiring experience. This book includes a section, "Where to View Alaska's Mammals," that describes many excellent vantage points; most are easily accessible. At Eklutna Lake in Chugach State Park, just an hour's drive from Anchorage, you can have a family picnic while watching Dall sheep on the mountainside. There's also plenty of wildlife to be seen from cars along Alaska's roads and from ferries on the Alaska Marine Highway. Cruise ships pass through a rich marine environment, while many smaller vessels specialize in wildlife tours. Flightseeing is popular throughout Alaska, and the pilots know where to find animals.

The section on wildlife viewing also includes several remote but remarkable places, such as the Pribilof Islands in the Bering Sea, where as many as a million northern fur seals haul out during the summer mating season. Over 10,000 bull walrus haul out for the summer at Bristol Bay's Round Island. Both locations are accessible by plane.

Outside Alaska, humans have disturbed and ultimately usurped much of the habitat that animals need to survive. Alaska is so vast and sparsely populated that most land mammals continue to thrive. The fate of Alaska's marine mammals is determined by the health and well-being of international waters. It's disturbing to note that Steller sea lion populations have plummeted 70 percent in the past decade, yet encouraging to report that gray whales have been removed from the Endangered Species List. Now, migrating gray whales once again mark the return of spring for some people along the coast of Alaska.

I took a boat cruise one cold, wet April day to Kenai Fjords National Park specifically to see the gray whales as they move up the coast. Each time we spotted a whale, people rushed from the boat's cabin out onto the deck to get a better view and hear the whale's whoosh and sigh as it exhaled, sending a spout of mist into the dank air. Long after the whale disappeared into the depths, we were still smiling over the scene we had just witnessed. An unerring instinct guides the gray whales thousands of miles on their spring migration from Mexico to Alaska. This book gives testimony to the equally strong force that draws us all to whales and to the other intriguing mammals of the Far North.

Female brown bear (right) and her two cubs wait to fish for salmon in the intertidal zone of Mikfik Creek, McNeil River State Game Sanctuary.

LAND MAMMALS

ARCTIC FOX

Most of Alaska's arctic foxes are brown gray in summer, white in winter. White fur provides not only camouflage in winter, but also additional warmth. A pigment called melanin gives the fox its brown-gray summer coat, but there's no melanin in white fur. Instead of being filled with the pigment, which conducts cold air, the hair cells of white fur are hollow. They trap warm air radiating from the fox and help protect the animal from the arctic cold.

There is also a color phase of arctic fox that is blue gray in color, both summer and winter. This fox, much less common than the fox that turns white in winter, is most often seen in the Pribilof and Aleutian islands. Both phases, however, are members of the same species.

Arctic foxes have short legs, a short muzzle, and a chubby, compact body—adaptations that conserve body heat. The less body area exposed to cold, the warmer the animal. The ears of an arctic fox are small, rounded, and almost completely covered by fur. In contrast, the desert kit fox has large, pointed ears with short hair. The ears of a kit fox dissipate heat; the ears of an arctic fox conserve it.

Arctic foxes make their dens in sandy ridges or well-drained soil on riverbanks. Dens may extend 6 to 12 feet underground and have an average of 4 entrances. An arctic fox often uses the same den year after year. An accumulation of bones, waste, and scat enriches the soil near dens so that they tend to stand out, an oasis of green in an otherwise drab landscape.

Summer is a frantic season for arctic foxes. Females give birth in May or June, and both parents help raise the pups. The parents hunt for up to 19 hours a day during summer.

Arctic foxes are accomplished scavengers. They find fish that wash up on the ocean shore and spawned-out arctic char in freshwater streams. A washed-up whale carcass can draw dozens of foxes, which tunnel into the whale until it resembles a piece of Swiss cheese.

In winter, the arctic fox probably ranges more widely than any other terrestrial animal. One fox tagged in Russia followed the winter pack ice across the Bering Strait and was captured a year later near Wainwright, Alaska. Arctic foxes frequently follow polar bears because a well-fed bear eats only the blubber from seals it kills, leaving feasts for foxes.

DID YOU KNOW?

ARCTIC FOX:
Changes in the length of day (hours of daylight)—and not changes in temperature—trigger molt and color alteration in the arctic fox.

◆ **SIZE AND COLOR:** Average length 43 inches, including 15-inch tail; 9 to 12 inches tall at shoulders; 5 to 9 pounds. Brown gray in summer, white in winter. One form is blue gray year-round.

◆ **REPRODUCTION:** Mate in March/early April. Average litter of 7 born after 52-day gestation. Birth weight 3 to 5 ounces.

◆ **LIFE SPAN:** about 4 years; 8 to 10 years maximum.

◆ **FOOD:** Lemmings, hares, birds, eggs, berries, carrion.

◆ **PREDATORS:** Wolves, polar bears, golden eagles, snowy owls, humans.

◆ **HABITAT AND RANGE:** Treeless tundra in coastal areas, plus pack ice in winter. Along the north and west coasts of Alaska to about 200 miles inland, and just as far offshore during winter freeze-up; also the Aleutian and Pribilof islands.

ARCTIC GROUND SQUIRREL

Hibernation is often described as a deep sleep, but hibernating arctic ground squirrels seem to be insomniacs. Brain-wave patterns show that the squirrel's brain remains active during hibernation. And every three weeks, the squirrel warms up to a normal body temperature, eliminates wastes, and then returns to hibernation.

Biologist Brian Barnes of the University of Alaska Fairbanks discovered that the body temperature of an arctic ground squirrel falls below freezing during hibernation. The exact process for this "supercooling" by the squirrel is not yet known. As the process becomes better understood, it could have practical implications for preservation of human organs for transplant.

Male arctic ground squirrels come out of hibernation in April and promptly compete with one another for the territories offering the best food supply and den sites with loose soils and good drainage. The females awaken a few weeks later. Each female scouts for the best possible territory and mates with the male who occupies it.

Grizzly bears spend a lot of time and energy hunting ground squirrels. The bear gives chase, the ground squirrel dives into its den, the grizzly tries to dig it out. This can be a futile exercise for the bear, because dens have many entrances and chambers. But some grizzlies have learned that ground squirrels are skittish; if there's enough commotion upstairs, a ground squirrel will often panic and run. So a bear will dig, dig, dig, then lift its head and look around. If a squirrel runs, it's all over.

Squirrels chatter three times to warn one another when a fox or other ground predator approaches. They switch to chattering five times when the ground predator gets close. A single whistling note warns of hawks, eagles, and other aerial predators. Once a bird lands, the squirrels' alarm switches to the ground-predator warning of five chatters.

Females give alarm calls more often than males because most females in a colony of arctic ground squirrels are related. Though sounding the alarm may put the female at risk, the effort can save members of her own family. Males usually leave the home colony at the end of their first summer and settle in a new area, where other ground squirrels are competitors, not cooperative relatives. In this setting, a male will just silently disappear into his den at the first sign of danger.

DID YOU KNOW?

ARCTIC GROUND SQUIRREL:
Eskimos call ground squirrels *sik-sik*, which mimics the squirrel alarm call.

♦ **SIZE AND COLOR:** 13 to 19 inches long, including tail of 3 to 6 inches; usually 1 to 2 pounds (but adults at Prudhoe Bay weigh 4 to 5 pounds). Rusty yellowish, with back slightly darker than belly.
♦ **REPRODUCTION:** Mate in late May, with 5 to 10 young born 24 days later. Birth weight ¼ ounce.
♦ **LIFE SPAN:** 2 to 3 years.
♦ **FOOD:** Seeds, roots, bulbs, and stems of plants. Insects, bird eggs, and carrion, including other ground squirrels.
♦ **PREDATORS:** Foxes, golden eagles, hawks, weasels, grizzly bears, wolverines, lynx.
♦ **HABITAT AND RANGE:** Most common in mountainous terrain on slopes with loose soil and good drainage, but also found on tundra. Most of Alaska except Southeast and the western Seward Peninsula.

BEAVER

The beaver's internal clock goes awry during Alaska's long winter. In some parts of the beaver's northern range, the sun disappears for many days. North America's largest rodent responds by feeding, sleeping, and working on a 26- to 29-hour cycle.

Some beavers live in dens dug into the banks of rivers or lakes; others build lodges in ponds. Beaver lodges are quite comfortable in winter. Inside, the beavers carpet a ledge above water with twigs, grass, and wood chips. A typical lodge is about 12 feet in diameter, with a roof that rises several feet above the water. Thick walls of branches and sticks reinforced with mud and rocks protect the beavers inside from predators and the elements. Beavers come and go through an underwater entrance.

Beavers cache food for the winter by jabbing sticks and branches into the mud on the bottom of their pond in a central location known as a feed bed. They eat the bark and the cambium layer beneath the bark, but not the wood itself.

This nocturnal animal can remain underwater for 15 minutes, enough time to swim ½ mile or more. In winter, beavers breathe bubbles trapped beneath the ice, including bubbles from their own exhalations. Underwater, their eyes are protected by a set of transparent lids. Their ears and nose shut tightly. Flaps of skin close behind their buckteeth so they can chew without getting wood chips or water down their throat. A beaver's webbed hind feet help propel it at 5 miles per hour, and the tail acts as a rudder.

To cut down a tree, a beaver stands on its hind legs and leans back on its tail. The beaver tilts its head to the side, starts to chomp, and the chips fly. The beaver rings a tree until it topples, cutting through a 5-inch-thick tree in 3 minutes.

Beavers are slow and clumsy on land, easy prey for predators. One reason that beavers are such dedicated dam builders is that the ponds created by the dams offer refuge from predators. When beavers go ashore to feed, they don't go far from the water's edge. Once they deplete easily accessible food supplies, beavers go back to work on their dam and raise the water level until they can reach more trees without venturing far from shore.

Some dams are longer than a football field, 12 feet high, and 20 feet wide at the base. Construction is a family affair. A lodge typically houses 2 adults, 4 newborn kits, and 4 kits from the previous year. The dam must create a pond that is deep enough so that it doesn't freeze solid in winter.

DID YOU KNOW?

BEAVER:
Newborn kits can swim immediately after birth, but they're so fat, furry, and buoyant that they have difficulty submerging to get out of the underwater entrance of their lodge.

✦ **SIZE AND COLOR:** 3 to 4 feet long, including tail 9 to 10 inches long; 6 inches wide; 40 to 60 pounds. Brown.

✦ **REPRODUCTION:** Mate in January and February, with 1 to 6 kits (average of 4) born in late April or May. Birth weight 1 pound.

✦ **LIFE SPAN:** 10 to 12 years.

✦ **FOOD:** Bark and cambium from willows, poplars, birches, aspens; herbs, ferns, grasses.

✦ **PREDATORS:** Wolves, coyotes, wolverines, lynx, bears, humans.

✦ **HABITAT AND RANGE:** Streams and rivers near willows and poplars. Most of Alaska except nonforested areas along the north and northwest coast.

BLACK BEAR

Eighty percent or more of a black bear's diet consists of plants, but its full diet includes a variety of protein sources. Black bears in Southeast Alaska eat barnacles in tidewater pools. And studies show that black bears prey on moose calves early in the spring.

Most people associate spawning salmon with brown bears, but black bears also catch these fish. A black bear catches salmon with its mouth, then pins the fish with its paws before giving it a solid bite. Once the edge is taken off its hunger, a black bear will sometimes release male salmon in favor of females. The bear steps on the females until eggs squirt out, then laps up this especially nutritious delicacy.

A black bear's weight increases by about 20 percent between spring and fall; a well-fed black bear waddles into its winter den. There's an ongoing debate over whether bears "hibernate" or simply enter a phase of winter "dormancy." In any case, the bear's heart rate drops about 75 percent, its body temperature falls 7 degrees Fahrenheit, and its long winter nap solves the problem of how to survive when no food is available. Unseasonably warm winter weather—about 50 degrees—will usually rouse a few black bears from winter-long sleep. And as numerous researchers will attest, when a den is disturbed, the bear awakens and quickly becomes alert.

Cubs weighing ½ pound each are born in the den. By the time they emerge in the spring, cubs weigh about 5 pounds. In most areas, they remain with their mother for one summer and then disperse.

There are a number of ways to tell a black bear from a brown/grizzly bear, though it's not always as simple as it sounds. Color alone can be misleading since both types of bears come in many color phases, and the fur of a backlit black bear can have the same grizzled appearance as a grizzly's. A black bear is usually about 30 percent smaller than a grizzly, but size alone is not a sure indicator.

Grizzly bears have a prominent hump over their shoulders, are burlier and more massive than black bears, and have a wider forehead with a dished face. The black bear's facial profile with its straight nose is often the best means of distinguishing between the two types of bears.

DID YOU KNOW?

BLACK BEAR:
Though 95 percent of Alaska's black bears actually are black, some are cinnamon or tan—and a rare blue gray "glacier bear" can be found near Yakutat and the St. Elias Range.

◆ **SIZE AND COLOR:** Males average 5 feet long; 24 to 30 inches tall; 200 pounds (with some weighing up to 600 pounds). Females 20 to 30 percent smaller. Usually black.

◆ **REPRODUCTION:** Mate in June and early July. Cubs, usually twins, born in February or March. Birth weight 8 ounces.

◆ **LIFE SPAN:** 20 to 25 years.

◆ **FOOD:** Insects, berries, fish, grasses, aspen catkins, clover, carrion, garbage, moose calves.

◆ **PREDATORS:** Wolves, grizzly bears, other black bears, humans.

◆ **HABITAT AND RANGE:** Prefer open forests to thick timber; seasonally from alpine meadows to ocean beaches. Everywhere in Alaska except north of Brooks Range, far western Alaska, Seward Peninsula, Kodiak Island, and Admiralty, Baranof, and Chichagof islands in Southeast Alaska.

BROWN/GRIZZLY BEAR

Grizzly bears were long regarded as a subspecies of brown bear, but grizzlies and browns intermingle freely, and taxonomists now classify them as one: *Ursus arctos,* the brown bear. In any case, technical classifications tend to be somewhat academic in Alaska, where most people continue to refer to bears that live along the coast as brown bears and to inland brown bears as grizzlies.

The coastal brown bears are substantially larger than the inland grizzlies. The coastal bears, with a diet rich in salmon, take advantage of the milder coastal climate to continue feeding and growing while the bears in the colder inland areas have already denned for the winter.

In the Arctic, some bears den for as long as 7½ months. During the long winter nap, the bear's heart rate drops and body temperature decreases. Adult males are the first to leave dens in the spring, and females with newborn cubs are the last. During exceptionally mild winters on Kodiak Island, some male bears don't den at all.

Bears everywhere are known as opportunistic feeders, and Alaska's brown bears are no exception. They dig for clams on tidal flats on the Alaska Peninsula, and they've been seen scavenging a walrus carcass that washed ashore on the Seward Peninsula. The inland browns, the grizzlies, often spend hours grazing on grass and sedges and rarely prey on full-grown moose or other large mammals. A grizzly's diet is about 30 percent animal protein, 70 percent vegetation.

The brown/grizzly bear usually exhibits tougher behavior toward intruders than the black bear because the two species walked down different evolutionary paths. Black bears are creatures of the forest. They live in dense cover that provides concealment from predators. Sows send cubs scampering up trees at the first sign of danger. Adult black bears can climb too. But brown/grizzly bears evolved on the open tundra, with no trees or shrubs to conceal them. A sow couldn't send her cubs up a tree to safety. Thus the brown/grizzly bear developed a different response to intruders than the black bear. If a black bear is startled, it will probably flee. If a brown/grizzly is intruded upon at close range, it may choose an attack as its best defense.

DID YOU KNOW?

BROWN/GRIZZLY BEAR:
Brown bears can be fastidious feeders, delicately filleting salmon with one claw or nibbling berries one at a time.

◆ **SIZE AND COLOR:** Male coastal brown bears 7 to 9 feet long; 4 to 5 feet tall; 500 to 900 pounds, up to 1,400 pounds. Females 30 to 40 percent smaller. Male grizzlies (inland brown bears) 6 to 7 feet long; 3½ to 4½ feet tall; 300 to 500 pounds. Females smaller. Ranges from light blond to dark brown, occasionally black.

◆ **REPRODUCTION:** Mate in May and June. Cubs, usually twins, born in January and February. Birth weight less than 2 pounds.

◆ **LIFE SPAN:** Up to 34 years, although males average 22 years, females 26.

◆ **FOOD:** Berries, sedges, grasses, salmon, carrion, moose calves, caribou calves.

◆ **PREDATORS:** Other bears, humans; wolves prey on grizzly cubs.

◆ **HABITAT AND RANGE:** Prefer open areas; availability of food triggers movement from low elevations to alpine areas. Found throughout Alaska except for some islands.

CARIBOU

Caribou are the only member of the deer family in which both sexes grow antlers. Bull caribou have impressive racks: up to 5½ feet long and up to 3 feet wide, with many points and distinctive forward-facing shovels. Cows have spikes or branched antlers 12 to 18 inches long.

During the fall mating season, a bull's huge rack attracts cows and warns away other bulls. Once the rut is over, a bull's antlers are just cumbersome decorations. Bulls begin dropping their antlers in mid-October, and most bulls have lost their racks by the end of December. Bulls and cows remain together in herds throughout the winter. Pregnant cows keep their antlers until April or early May and use them as weapons to fend off males that try to bully them from feeding sites.

Cows give birth to a single 12-pound calf in May or June. The calf is extremely vulnerable to predators for the first few days of its life. If calving were staggered over a month or so, bears and wolves might systematically hunt and kill every new calf. Instead, all the cows in a herd give birth within 5 days of one another, in effect swamping the predators with too many calves. Still, 40 percent of new caribou calves born in Denali National Park and Preserve are killed by predators.

Alaska is home to about 25 fairly distinct herds of caribou, totaling some 1,000,000 animals. Caribou are called the nomads of the North because they're always on the move seeking food. Tens of thousands of animals migrate up to 900 miles between their winter range, spring calving ground, and summer feeding area. This constant movement prevents overgrazing.

Warble flies, bot flies, and mosquitoes plague the caribou. During the summer, when caribou have a short, thin coat of hair, these insects cause the animals to twitch, shake, stamp their feet, and finally burst into mad sprints across the tundra. During exceptionally bad bug years, caribou may go farther north than usual because windswept coastal areas have fewer insects.

Caribou regularly swim across rivers and streams during their migrations. The same hollow hair that insulates caribou from winter's cold provides flotation. The caribou's 5-inch-diameter hooves make good paddles. During the winter, the hooves serve as snowshoes for easy walking and as shovels for digging through snow to reach food.

DID YOU KNOW?

CARIBOU:
The caribou's most important adaptation to winter is its ability to smell lichens—its primary food—beneath the snow.

◆ **SIZE AND COLOR:** 6 to 7 feet long; 3½ to 4 feet tall at shoulders; males 350 to 400 pounds, females 175 to 225 pounds. Rich brown, with white belly; males have a silvery cape.

◆ **REPRODUCTION:** Peak breeding season in October. Single calf born in May or June. Birth weight 12 pounds.

◆ **LIFE SPAN:** 8 to 10 years.

◆ **FOOD:** Grasses, sedges, and leaves of willows and dwarf birches in summer. Lichens (reindeer moss) and dried sedges in winter.

◆ **PREDATORS:** Wolves, bears, humans; bears, wolves, and golden eagles prey on calves.

◆ **HABITAT AND RANGE:** Tundra; occasionally in forests during winter. Northern third of Alaska and the Alaska Peninsula, with scattered herds elsewhere in the state.

DALL SHEEP

Winter is a lean season for Dall sheep, as it is for many animals. Rich summer grasses are gone, and the sheep expend more energy getting to food than they derive from eating it. By winter's end, the sheep are living off fat reserves accumulated during the summer.

A cold winter is actually better for Dall sheep than a warm one. Cold weather brings light, powdery snow that's easily blown away by wind on south-facing hillsides, exposing food for the sheep. They can paw through the fluffy snow that remains to reach the vegetation beneath it.

In contrast, it's difficult for sheep to dig through the heavy, wet snow that accompanies warm weather. Worse, wet snow sets up like concrete when temperatures drop again. And cold temperatures after warm winter rains can create a layer of ice that seals vegetation from the sheep. The ice makes for slippery footing on steep slopes and leads to falls and broken bones.

Dall sheep grow a winter coat that is up to 8 inches long and 2 to 3 inches thick, a blanket of coarse, hollow hair that provides excellent insulation from the cold.

Winter takes a heavy toll on lambs and immature sheep. Lambs that survive the rigors of birth usually do fine their first summer, but all the food they eat is necessary for growth; they don't accumulate reserves of fat. Up to half of all lambs perish their first winter, and up to 20 percent of all 2-year-olds die for the same reason. Sheep that are 3 to 7 years old are in their prime; their winter mortality rate is only 4 percent. But old age is almost as deadly as youth; each winter, about one-quarter of all Dall sheep over the age of 7 die.

Both male and female Dall sheep grow horns, with the male's horns growing longer and heavier than the female's after the age of 3. Rams are 6 years old before their horns have a three-quarter curl and 7 or 8 years old by the time they have full-curl horns. A ram's horns are status symbols. Rams display their horns to one another to make a visual impression so that there is usually no need for actual combat.

Males and females live apart except during the mating season, which brings together small bands of males that have been scattered throughout the mountains. At this time, many individual rams engage in pitched battles. Two rams will rear up on their hind legs and charge each other, cracking heads with a sound like a big bat hitting the side of a barn door. Though males occasionally battle for possession of a female in estrus, most conflicts center around determining who stands where on the social ladder.

DID YOU KNOW?

DALL SHEEP:
Horns of the Dall sheep are made of keratin, the same material as in fingernails.

◆ **SIZE AND COLOR:** Rams 3 to 3½ feet tall at shoulders; 150 to 160 pounds. Ewes 110 to 130 pounds. White.
◆ **REPRODUCTION:** Mate from mid-November to early December. One lamb born in late May or early June. Birth weight 5 to 6 pounds.
◆ **LIFE SPAN:** 12 to 15 years.

◆ **FOOD:** Sedges, grasses, willows. Lichens in winter.
◆ **PREDATORS:** Wolves, humans; golden eagles occasionally prey on lambs.
◆ **HABITAT AND RANGE:** Open ridges and meadows near steep slopes. Mountains of central and northern Alaska.

HOARY MARMOT

Old-time Alaskans called marmots "whistlers." The marmot's high-pitched alarm call, sounding like a traffic cop's whistle, carries a mile or more through still mountain air. They whistle to warn their family about predators. Dall sheep, arctic ground squirrels, and smart hikers know that the marmot's warning call could signal the approach of a grizzly bear. In addition to their warning whistle, marmots yip, yell, bark, and hiss.

All four feet of the hoary marmot are black, which helps explain its Latin name, *Marmota caligata* (*caligata* means "boots"). Much like a grizzly bear, these marmots have hoary, grizzled fur that's frosted with gray. The fur blends in well with rocks; when predators approach, marmots flatten themselves atop rocks or dive for cover into their underground dens.

Hoary marmots, the most common of the three marmot species in Alaska, live at or above timberline in dens located near extensive boulder fields or rock slides. Every marmot colony has numerous dens connected by a network of well-worn trails. Spur trails lead to feeding sites.

Dens are protected by boulders so large a grizzly can't move them or by clusters of rocks embedded in the soil so that wolverines and bears can't dig into the den. A grizzly will excavate huge mounds of dirt and rock in what usually proves to be a fruitless attempt to dig marmots out of a den. Golden eagles pose the greatest threat to marmots, especially the young ones.

There is usually a lookout point above a den or within 10 yards of it. When a marmot sights a predator, its sharp whistle is quickly relayed throughout the marmot community.

Marmots are social animals that live in colonies of a dozen or more animals. The young remain with their family for 2 years, sometimes longer. Marmots are not territorial; there's no dominance hierarchy, and conflict is rare. When family members meet, they appear to kiss, although they're really just identifying one another by scent. Pairs of males often stand up on their hind legs, put their front paws on each other's shoulders, and playfully wrestle.

Mosquitoes can drive marmots into their dens. Marmots love to sun on warm rocks, but they have to find a breezy spot to keep pesky insects to a tolerable level. You'll see more marmots when it's breezy and overcast than on a calm, sunny day.

Marmots feast during Alaska's brief summer. By autumn, mature marmots are almost as wide as they are long. When winter arrives, they hibernate for 7 to 9 months, sleeping soundly in the womb of the mountains.

DID YOU KNOW?

HOARY MARMOT:
Marmots are not strict vegetarians. They eat grasshoppers and bird eggs when available.

◆ **SIZE AND COLOR:** 24 to 30 inches long, including 7- to 10-inch tail; 8 to 20 pounds. Gray over shoulders, honey-brown on flanks, black feet, black band over nose; grizzled appearance.

◆ **REPRODUCTION:** Mate in April and May, with 4 to 6 young born after 5-week gestation. Birth weight 1½ ounces.

◆ **LIFE SPAN:** 10 years or more.

◆ **FOOD:** Grasses, forbs, flowers, roots.

◆ **PREDATORS:** Wolverines, wolves, red foxes, coyotes, grizzly bears, golden eagles.

◆ **HABITAT AND RANGE:** Base of talus slopes. Most mountainous areas.

LYNX

While it's unusual for people to see the secretive lynx, this is the one member of the cat family that's common in Alaska. At first glance, lynx look a little out of proportion: the feet are too big for the legs, the legs are too long for the body, the body is too small for the foundation beneath it. Based on size alone, the tracks of a much bigger cat, the mountain lion, would be difficult to distinguish from the tracks of a lynx. Both have paws that are 3 to 4½ inches in width and 4 inches long.

The lynx, however, has the perfect physique for traveling in deep snow. Large feet in combination with a lightweight body help prevent the lynx from sinking deeply in snow, and long legs power the animal through snow when it's chasing prey.

Lynx dine primarily on snowshoe hares. Mice aren't big enough to sustain them; arctic ground squirrels and marmots hibernate all winter (and lynx do not). Lynx hunt ptarmigan, grouse, and other birds that winter in Alaska, but they get only an occasional opportunity to pounce on a bird before it flies away. Dall sheep and caribou are usually too big for the lynx. So lynx have evolved as specialist predators, and their specialty is snowshoe hares.

A lynx catches prey by stalking and pouncing. If the chase isn't over quickly, the lynx loses. They're sprinters, not endurance runners. They rely on stealth to get close to hares, and startling quickness to catch them. A hare will leap to the left, veer to the right, and reverse direction—and as often as not, the lynx stays with it, with the chase ending in an explosion of snow.

Hare populations are cyclical, building and building only to crash every 8 to 12 years. The lynx population follows suit. When hares are abundant, female lynx breed their first year and have large litters. When the hare population is low, some lynx don't breed at all; those that do have small litters.

When hares are scarce, lynx disperse widely and attack prey they usually ignore. The lynx's teeth and jaws are too small to effectively grasp large mammals. But they can catch foxes in deep snow. Lynx will leap on Dall sheep from rocky ledges and rake their eyes to make the sheep vulnerable so the lynx can overpower them.

Lynx don't require an elaborate den. A female will den in a hollow log, a shallow cave in a cliff, or even beneath a log in a thick brush pile. Lynx kittens sound like loud house cats.

DID YOU KNOW?

LYNX:
Lynx are good swimmers.

* **SIZE AND COLOR:** 36 to 40 inches long, including 4-inch tail; 24 to 28 inches tall at shoulders; 18 to 38 pounds. Males slightly bigger than females. Buff gray.
* **REPRODUCTION:** Mate in March and April, with 1 to 4 kits born after 63-day gestation. Birth weight 7 ounces.
* **LIFE SPAN:** 11 years maximum, but few live past 5.
* **FOOD:** Snowshoe hares (almost exclusively); ptarmigan, grouse, waterfowl, ground squirrels, red squirrels, mice, (rarely) Dall sheep.
* **PREDATORS:** Humans, occasionally wolves, wolverines; wolves, coyotes, foxes, wolverines, raptors prey on kittens.
* **HABITAT AND RANGE:** Hardwood and spruce forests. Most of the state except Southeast Alaska and far western coast.

MARTEN

Martens are house-cat-size members of the weasel family with soft, dense fur and a long, fluffy tail. With a short face and erect, rounded ears like those of a fox, martens look inquisitive and always seem nervous. They give a low, rasping growl when angry or curious, which is most of the time, and they bound and dash quickly through the forest.

Martens have sharp nonretractable claws that are good for climbing trees or grasping prey. Mice and voles are their primary food. A marten will immediately drag its prey—whether mouse or vole, hare or squirrel—into a thicket or some other cover to protect itself from attack by a predator while it is feeding.

Also important on the Alaskan marten's menu are berries: crowberries, cranberries, and blueberries. During the peak of the blueberry season, martens eat so many berries that their lips are tinged with blue, and even their scat turns blue.

In Alaska, martens are most common in mature conifer or mixed-wood forests in the Interior. Like many animals, they prefer the edges of the forest and often travel along streams and lakeshores. In Southeast Alaska, martens scavenge the beaches for food.

Martens always try to stay near trees. They travel on the ground, but zip up trees to pursue squirrels and birds or to escape from large predators. If a marten has to cross an open bog or swamp, it will travel beneath every available tree.

Like squirrels, martens can reverse their hind feet and come down trees headfirst. Their legs pivot around at the hips so that on the way down from a tree, they can grip with the rear paws. They can leap 9 feet horizontally between trees and jump as far as 20 feet to the ground without injury. On calm, cool days, a marten will sleep stretched out on a tree limb.

Martens are territorial, with both males and females having a territory 5 to 10 miles in diameter. Male martens are polygamous, and one male's territory will overlap the territories of three or four females.

Martens cover about 5 miles per day in an erratic manner, investigating any sound, movement, or smell that suggests food. Their curiosity leads them up every inclined log they encounter, a trait that makes them easy to trap. One researcher, using strawberry jam as bait in a live trap, captured the same marten 77 times.

DID YOU KNOW?

MARTEN:
The marten preys heavily on red squirrels throughout most of its range in the Lower 48, but not in Alaska.

◆ **SIZE AND COLOR:** Males 19 to 25 inches long, including 5- to 9-inch tail; 2 to 3 pounds. Females 30 percent smaller. Brown with creamy yellow or orange patch on chest and neck.

◆ **REPRODUCTION:** Mate in July and August, with 3 young born in April or May. Birth weight 1 ounce.

◆ **LIFE SPAN:** 10 years.

◆ **FOOD:** Voles, mice, berries, small birds, eggs, vegetation, nuts, insects, red squirrels, snowshoe hares, carrion.

◆ **PREDATORS:** Lynx, coyotes, red foxes, hawks, owls, eagles, humans.

◆ **HABITAT AND RANGE:** Trees are the critical element in their habitat. Most of Alaska except the treeless tundra of northern and western Alaska.

MOOSE

Female moose control events during the autumn mating season. It's common to see one big bull in the company of many cows, but that doesn't necessarily mean he's the herd-master with a harem of eager females. Look carefully and you'll notice bulls on the sidelines. The big bull is fending them off because the cows—when they're ready—will mate with other selected bulls. Overzealous bull moose constantly make advances toward cows that have not yet come into estrus. The cows ignore or rebuff them. A cow might lay her ears back, raise her hackles, and keep her backside away from the bull. But this doesn't dissuade all bulls. There are times when a cow moose literally kicks a male in the head to get the message across.

When a cow moose approaches estrus, she stakes out a small area and begins calling to bulls. A bull courting a cow becomes territorial, urinating to mark boundaries, calling with a bellowing roar, and thrashing brush with his antlers. At this time, evenly matched bulls may have serious fights that tear up the turf and snap small trees. The weapons are antlers that, on outsize bulls, can reach a width of 81 inches and weigh 70 pounds.

Battles between bulls are more often ritualistic. They rock their antlers at each other and dip their heads to display their weaponry, hoping to win the war without fighting a battle. This works when there's a size disparity between contestants. A young bull will leave without a fight. But he won't go far. He will wait, and watch, and if the big bull moves away to settle a dispute with another rival, the young bull will quickly mate with a willing cow. The bulls shed their antlers each year following mating season; cows don't have antlers.

Cinnamon-colored calves are born the following spring. They grow at a phenomenal rate: calves that weigh 35 pounds at birth reach weights of 300 to 400 pounds by autumn. A mother moose with calves is best avoided; they're quick to charge people who approach too closely.

Moose relish fresh grass in the early summer, but have difficulty reaching it. Their legs are too long, their neck too short. They feed by kneeling awkwardly, their bulbous nose to the ground and their rump in the air, with their little 2- to 4-inch-long tail visible. Their big ears swivel like periscopes as they listen for predators.

DID YOU KNOW?

MOOSE:
"Velvet" covering the antlers is laced with blood capillaries which provide nutrients to the growing antlers; velvet is shed prior to the rut.

◆ **SIZE AND COLOR:** Males 6½ to 7 feet tall at shoulders; 1,200 to 1,600 pounds. Females 800 to 1,300 pounds. Brown.

◆ **REPRODUCTION:** Peak of mating season in late September, with 1 to 3 calves born in late May or early June. Birth weight 28 to 35 pounds.

◆ **LIFE SPAN:** Usually less than 16 years.

◆ **FOOD:** Willow leaves and grasses in summer; twigs and branches of willows, dwarf birches, aspens, cottonwoods, alders in winter.

◆ **PREDATORS:** Wolves, bears, humans, occasionally transient killer whales (when moose swim sea channels).

◆ **HABITAT AND RANGE:** Areas with willow and birch trees, often along river drainages; also on timberline plateaus. Throughout Alaska as far south as the Stikine River in Southeast, as far north as the Colville River in the Arctic.

MOUNTAIN GOAT

Contrary to popular belief, mountain goats don't have hooves like suction cups. Each hoof is split, allowing a goat's "toes" to spread wider than the hoof is long. Each hoof's hard outer rim surrounds what can be described as a protruding traction pad. This design gives the goat gripping power.

Goats also have bodies that are built for climbing cliffs. They're slab-sided, instead of rounded like deer or Dall sheep. This body form allows them to move along narrow ledges. They have massive front quarters but relatively small hindquarters, giving them power for pulling up with their front legs rather than the speed that comes from pushing off with the rear legs. Goats can't outrun predators, but they escape by climbing steep cliffs.

A study near Ketchikan found that wintering mountain goats spent most of their time on cliffs with a 50 to 65 percent slope. (The stairs in a typical house have a slope of 30 to 35 percent.) Goats often find themselves in difficult spots, and then subtle signs of fear and stress are noticeable. They flatten their ears, raise their tail, crouch a bit, and flick their tongue past their lips. A nanny with a kid stays on the downhill side of the kid to guard it against falls. She rarely allows her kid to wander more than 30 feet away.

Predators have their eyes on mountain goats. Eagles occasionally swoop down on kids and try to knock them off cliffs.

Wolves hunt adults that descend into the low country, and grizzly bears pose a threat. But winter brings the gravest danger to mountain goats, threatening them with avalanches, starvation, and deadly falls due to snow and ice.

Goats don't have a fixed territory, but they do have a dominance hierarchy based on the ability to defend personal space. Aggressive behavior is a daily constant, and many serious injuries result from one goat forcing another off a cliff. Male goats don't go head to head in battles with their 7- to 10-inch stilettolike horns. Instead, they strike at each other's rumps, which have thick skin. Females have horns too, but they're slimmer than the male's.

For most of the year, males and females live apart from each other. When males begin mingling with females during the fall rut, females fear and avoid them. Males solve the problem by crouching, crawling on their belly, and displaying other subordinate postures. In time, a female learns to tolerate her groveling companion, and a new generation is conceived.

DID YOU KNOW?

MOUNTAIN GOAT:
Goat kids and marmots sometimes follow each other and sleep side by side.

♦ **SIZE AND COLOR:** Males 4 to 5¾ feet long; 3 to 3½ feet tall at shoulders; 190 to 280 pounds. Females 130 to 190 pounds. Off-white with a yellowish tinge.
♦ **REPRODUCTION:** Mate in November and December. Single kid born in May or early June. Birth weight 6½ pounds.
♦ **LIFE SPAN:** 12 to 15 years.
♦ **FOOD:** Grasses, herbs, shrubs, hemlocks, mosses, lichens.
♦ **PREDATORS:** Wolves, grizzly bears, humans; golden eagles prey on kids.
♦ **HABITAT AND RANGE:** Steep mountain slopes; broken terrain featuring cliffs. From Southeast Alaska along coast to Cook Inlet; Chugach and Talkeetna mountains; isolated band in eastern Alaska Range.

MUSK OX

The musk ox is an Ice Age relic that once lived beside the mammoth and the woolly rhinoceros. One reason that musk oxen outlasted their companions is their habit of forming a defensive ring to fend off predators—a strategy that proved suicidal when men armed with rifles arrived in the Alaskan Arctic and simply gunned down entire herds of the animals. They were killed for food or sport and in some cases to get the young for zoos. In 1865, Alaska's last 13 musk oxen were shot.

In 1930, the United States purchased 34 musk oxen from Greenland, and they were eventually moved to Nunivak Island in the Bering Sea, where they thrived. Musk oxen were later reintroduced to most of their original Alaska range.

The musk ox's most noticeable feature is its long guard hairs, which form a skirt that almost drags on the ground. Guard hairs on the neck of a bull musk ox are 24 inches long. Inupiat Eskimos call the musk ox *oomingmak*, the "bearded one."

Beneath the guard hairs is a dense, soft, light underfur called *qiviut* that helps the musk ox stay warm at temperatures that drive polar bears and arctic foxes to shelter. Eskimos wove qiviut into mosquito netting, and today qiviut is knitted into warm, and expensive, garments.

During extremely cold weather, musk oxen stand still to conserve energy. They're stoic in the face of harsh conditions.

They paw through snow with their front hooves to obtain grass and other vegetation.

When musk oxen are pursued by predators, they often display the unusual habit of maintaining body contact when running. They gallop shoulder to shoulder, flank to flank, moving like a single animal, flowing like a wave over the tundra.

During the mating season, battles between males follow a ritual which can be broken off at any stage. First one bull lowers its head and rubs a scent gland near its eye on its extended foreleg. Next it rakes the ground with its horns. Then one animal moves toward the other, eyes averted and head tipped to show its horns. If the conflict continues to escalate, the bulls engage in a shoving match. During an all-out battle, they will charge, crashing into each other.

During the rut, male musk oxen secrete a substance in their urine that has a sweet, pungent smell. You can even smell it on their breath. Although the musk ox usually exhibits a calm demeanor, tensions run high during the rut. An observer saw one agitated bull leap clear off the ground in what looked like an attempt to hook the floats of a low-flying airplane.

DID YOU KNOW?

MUSK OX:
Sparring bull musk oxen crash head-on with the force of an automobile smashing into a brick wall at 17 miles per hour.

- SIZE AND COLOR: Males 6 to 8 feet long; 5 feet tall at shoulders; average 600 pounds. Females 4 feet tall; 350 pounds. Dark brown, with creamy patches on muzzle, forehead, legs, saddle.
- REPRODUCTION: Mate in September. Single calf born in April or May. Birth weight 19 pounds.

- LIFE SPAN: 20 years.
- FOOD: Grasses, sedges, forbs, willows, lichens.
- PREDATORS: Wolves, grizzly bears, humans.
- HABITAT AND RANGE: Open arctic tundra. Nunivak Island, Nelson Island, scattered herds along northern coast.

PIKA

Once you've heard a pika's warning call and seen the creature that makes it, you won't forget either one. A pika looks like a guinea pig and sounds like a kazoo. One biologist described the pika's call as a nasal *yink* or *yank*. Others say it sounds like a sharp bark or the squeak of a rubber toy. But whether you'd describe the call as a chirp, a whistle, or a bleat, one thing is certain—it's odd and memorable.

There are 19 species of pikas worldwide, and one of these species is Alaska's collared pika, so called because of the light-grayish "collar" of hair around its neck and shoulders. The pika is related to rabbits and hares. But pikas have short, dish-shaped ears, and they don't have a fluffy tail. In fact, they don't have a tail at all, though they do have a tailbone just beneath the skin.

Pikas are gregarious in that several of them will live in the same general area, but each pika has its own ½-acre territory. They mark territorial boundaries with urine, dung, and a scent gland on their face. The urine and dung are probably meant to ward off trespassers, while the facial scent attracts members of the opposite sex. Pikas are rarely found more than 20 yards from rocky, talus slopes. But since they feed on vegetation, most territories are at the edge of rock piles rather than in the center.

Pikas don't hibernate, so beginning in midsummer they

begin caching food for the winter. A pika cuts plants, carries them crosswise in its mouth back to the rocks, and builds a stack about 2 feet high and 2 feet in diameter. The pika works at a frantic pace, making about one trip a minute from the cache to a feeding area.

During winter, the pika lives comfortably in a maze of tunnels beneath the snow, with routes leading to its cache of vegetation. After months of darkness and silence, pikas are extremely paranoid when they first emerge into the Alaskan spring. When they see the shadow of a golden eagle passing overhead, pikas give a sharp warning call. They warn one another about all predators except weasels, which are small enough to pursue pikas into their rocky world of cracks and crevices. When a weasel appears, a pika will not warn its neighbors because that might call attention to itself. Instead, it quietly disappears into the rocks. It's every pika for itself.

DID YOU KNOW?

PIKA:
A single pika will usually cache about 12 pounds of food for the winter, but an occasional pika will create a giant stack of winter food that weighs as much as 50 pounds.

* **SIZE AND COLOR:** 6 to 8 inches long; 4 to 5 ounces. Grayish brown, with light "collar" around neck and shoulders, white patch on chest, white belly and feet.
* **REPRODUCTION:** Mate in spring. Litter of 2 to 6 born after 30-day gestation. Then mate again, with second litter of 2 to 6 arriving early in July. Birth weight ⅓ ounce.
* **LIFE SPAN:** 3 years.
* **FOOD:** Forbs, grasses, flowers, seeds, lupines.
* **PREDATORS:** Hawks, weasels, eagles.
* **HABITAT AND RANGE:** Rock slides and talus slopes near meadows or patches of vegetation in mountainous terrain. From Mount McKinley and Alaska Range south and east through Wrangell Mountains and St. Elias Range to White Pass near Skagway.

PORCUPINE

Porcupines have an admirable equanimity about them. When approached by an assailant, porcupines simply gnash and chatter their teeth and rattle their tails, then resume their business. They'll climb a tree if one is available—anything to avoid a fight. The porcupine's quills, all 30,000 of them, are a last line of defense.

These quills are stiff, filled with a foamlike core, and barbed like a fish hook. They vary in length from 2½ to 4½ inches and are loosely attached to the porcupine's skin. When attacked, a porcupine turns away from its tormentor and lifts the skin on its back, presenting the attacker with a forest of quills. The porcupine does not throw its quills; it flips its tail up to drive the quills into its enemy. Once quills are embedded, the fish-hook design makes it difficult—and painful—to pull them out. Every muscle contraction drives them deeper into the body. You can use pliers to remove quills from the nose of a dog unfortunate enough to interfere with a porcupine. If there are many quills or they are deeply embedded, it may take the help of a veterinarian who can anesthetize the dog.

Despite the quills, porcupines are able to manage mating and birthing with no special problems. The quills of a newborn porcupine—called a porcupette—are soft during delivery and harden within ½ hour of birth.

Porcupines dine on plants and flowers. But during the lean winter season, they eat the cambium layer—the soft inner bark—of trees. This can have disastrous consequences for the tree. The cambium carries moisture and minerals to leaves and branches, which then send sugar and starch back down to the trunk and roots. Sugar concentrates just above the scarred spot where the porcupines have been eating. Porcupines then return again and again to indulge their sweet tooth. If they completely girdle the tree with their eating, the tree dies.

Porcupines also crave salt because their vegetarian diet is low in sodium. Hikers have had their sweat-soaked pack straps or leather boots turned into porcupine food.

Athabascan Indians of the Interior still dye porcupine quills with local vegetable materials and sew them onto animal-skin clothing or use them in making earrings and other decorative items. Quills can be obtained by tapping a porcupine lightly on its back with a long-handled piece of Styrofoam and later removing the quills from the material.

DID YOU KNOW?

PORCUPINE:
Porcupines are good swimmers and will graze on plants in shallow water.

♦ **SIZE AND COLOR:** 23 to 39 inches long, including 7- to 9-inch tail; up to 12 inches tall at shoulders; 15 to 28 pounds. Black or brownish black, with yellow tinge from quills.

♦ **REPRODUCTION:** Mate in September and October. Single offspring born in April or May. Birth weight 1 to 2 pounds.

♦ **LIFE SPAN:** 5 to 7 years.
♦ **FOOD:** Most lush, green plants and flowers; in winter, inner bark (cambium layer) of trees.

♦ **PREDATORS:** Wolves, wolverines, lynx, foxes, coyotes, bears, owls.

♦ **HABITAT AND RANGE:** Forested areas. All of Alaska except Seward Peninsula and north of Brooks Range.

RED FOX

In February and March, when most other animals are struggling to survive Alaska's long winter, red foxes begin courting. Your nose will tell you when the foxes' mating season has begun; their urine takes on a pungent, musky odor, and a mildly skunky smell permeates their territory. Males and females that have led solitary lives now form pairs and begin traveling together.

Courtship lasts 6 to 8 weeks. The female (vixen) readies several dens; she will move her family if a site is disturbed. Red foxes sometimes make use of abandoned wolf dens, but more often they enlarge the dens of marmots, arctic ground squirrels, and other burrowing animals.

Kits are charcoal gray at birth except for a white-tipped tail. At first, the vixen stays inside with her kits. But after 2 weeks, she begins to hunt again.

Although red foxes trot at a steady 6 miles per hour and sprint in excess of 30, they don't run down prey as coyotes and wolves do. Instead, they pounce on it. A red fox will stalk a mouse, then spring 3 feet into the air and come back down, using its forefeet to pin the mouse.

The kits begin fighting with one another 25 days after birth. These are serious fights. Over the next 10 days, the kits establish a strict hierarchy. The dominant kit lords it over his or her siblings and through intimidation or brute force gets all the food it wants. The parents don't interfere. If food is limited, the runt of the litter is the first to perish. This keeps the litter size in line with the resources of the parents' territory.

Parents visit the den less and less as summer goes on, and the youngsters begin to explore on their own. At first they travel in groups of two or three, but they quickly learn it's difficult for three foxes to stalk one mouse. Eventually they hunt alone.

A red fox on the move struggles to balance its high level of curiosity with a wariness that borders on paranoia. A red fox doesn't like to approach any foreign object that it hasn't seen from all sides. The fox will circle, look things over, and test the wind to catch any enticing or alarming scents. If there's no scent, or the view doesn't reveal enough information, the fox departs.

DID YOU KNOW?

RED FOX:
In areas where the ranges of red foxes and arctic foxes overlap, the dominant red foxes dig arctic foxes from their dens and kill them.

SIZE AND COLOR: 33 to 43 inches long, including 11- to 18-inch tail; 15 to 16 inches tall at shoulders; 6 to 15 pounds, males heavier than females. Three color phases: red, silver, and cross-color. Most common color is red, with white chest and underparts, black legs, white-tipped tail.

REPRODUCTION: Mate in February and March, with 4 to 10 kits born after gestation of 53 days. At birth, 8 inches long and 4 to 5 ounces.

LIFE SPAN: 3 to 7 years.

FOOD: Voles and mice; also hares, squirrels, insects, birds, eggs, berries.

PREDATORS: Wolves, coyotes, lynx, wolverines, bears, humans; golden eagles prey on kits.

HABITAT AND RANGE: Broken country with hills and draws; lowland marshes. Most of Alaska except western Aleutian Islands and some islands in Prince William Sound and Southeast Alaska.

RIVER OTTER

River otters start swimming when they're 7 to 8 weeks old, and a pup's first encounter with water tends to be traumatic. A mother often begins swimming lessons by entering the water and calling to her young. If need be, a female will drag a reluctant pup into the water by the scruff of its neck. Sometimes she will let the youngster hang on as she swims out into deep water, where she shakes it off. It's sink or swim, and the pup quickly discovers it can swim.

The family then begins traveling on a regular circuit that takes 1 to 4 weeks to complete. Pups are weaned at 5 months and stay with their mother until just before she gives birth again. The traveling otters rest in riverbank burrows, abandoned muskrat dens, or the bases of hollow trees.

Their route, which usually follows rivers, lakes, streams, and the edges of bays, may take them several miles overland. This is when their principal predators—wolves, coyotes, and lynx—can get at them. Sometimes the otters walk, other times they bound. They can run as fast as a person. Otters slide down banks and into the water by taking a running start, tucking their front legs backward at their sides, extending their hind legs behind them, and then belly flopping.

Unlike their relative the sea otter, which stays in saltwater, Alaska's river otters hunt in both freshwater and saltwater.

Otters dive for prey. They can stay down for 3 to 4 minutes and swim ¼ mile between breaths. At slow speeds, otters swim by steering with their tail and stroking with their webbed hind feet. They swim fast by flexing their body in an undulating motion that carries them along at 6 miles an hour. During winter, otters breathe the air in bubbles trapped beneath the ice.

Their eyes are located high on the skull, and thus they can swim with most of their body submerged and still see above water. On their body, guard hairs an inch long cover a dense underfur that's ¼ inch thick. Otters have a flexible spine; they can bend forward or sideways and form a complete circle. They have a serpentine yet muscular appearance.

Otters hiss and snarl when angry or frightened. A birdlike chirp indicates anxiety, most often when family members become separated. They grunt when feeding, mumble together during gatherings, and explode "hah!" when alarmed. Throughout the day, they wrestle, play tag or hide and seek, and manipulate sticks, rocks, and other objects that capture their interest. The only time they sit still and keep quiet is when they're sleeping, which is about half the day.

DID YOU KNOW?

RIVER OTTER:
On packed snow, a river otter can bound, flop, and slide, hitting a speed of 15 miles per hour.

◆ **SIZE AND COLOR:** 35 to 54 inches long, including 11- to 20-inch tail; 9 to 10 inches tall at shoulders; 11 to 33 pounds. Females 25 percent smaller than males. Dark brown that looks black when wet.

◆ **REPRODUCTION:** Mate in May, with 1 to 6 pups (usually 2 or 3) born 9 to 13 months later. Birth weight 1 pound.

◆ **LIFE SPAN:** 10 to 15 years.
◆ **FOOD:** Fish, snails, mussels, clams, crabs, occasional birds or mammals, some plants.
◆ **PREDATORS:** Wolves, coyotes, lynx, humans.
◆ **HABITAT AND RANGE:** Rivers, streams, lakes, bays. Most of Alaska except the Aleutians and north of Brooks Range.

SHORT-TAILED WEASEL

Alaska's short-tailed weasels are about 15 percent larger than the short-tailed weasels found in some areas of the Lower 48 states. Some believe they are bigger in northern latitudes because their prey is bigger.

These weasels are deadly predators. They have to be. They have a long, skinny, "snakelike" body that dissipates heat, but unlike snakes, they live in a cold climate. They need a lot of fuel to keep warm. They eat one-third to one-half their body weight each day.

Weasels are a scourge on burrowing animals because their body fits into any hole that their head can slip into. The weasel's head is wedge-shaped (like that of a rattlesnake) and only about 1¼ inches wide, with exceptionally large jaw muscles. Weasels bite their prey at the base of the neck, grab it with their front feet, and rake it with their hind feet. They start eating the prey on the spot, but when their hunger is slaked, they drag the carcass back to their den. A weasel can drag prey that weighs more than ten times its own weight. Weasels cache food, and dens often include a side tunnel for storing mice and other prey.

Weasels are bold and inquisitive. On hunting excursions, they walk and bound this way and that to investigate any sight, sound, or smell that might mean food. A weasel may cover 2 or

3 miles just in traveling to a point that's only 800 feet from its den.

Alaska's short-tailed weasels are white in the winter and brown in the summer. (These animals also are sometimes known as ermines.) The amount of daylight triggers a molt that determines color. As the days get longer in spring, the weasel sheds its white winter fur, and the pituitary gland stimulates production of a brown pigment in its new summer coat. Brown fur appears first on the back of the neck. As the molt continues, more brown fur appears on the shoulder blades and down the back. Lastly, the throat and belly turn a creamy off-white.

The process is reversed as the amount of light decreases in autumn. Now the pituitary gland inhibits the release of pigment, and the animal's brown fur turns white, except for the tip of its tail, which is black, with hairs 1½ inches long, compared with only ½ inch on the rest of the body. This color scheme is a diversion. Predators tend to strike at the weasel's tail rather than its body. If they're the least bit off target and strike behind the ermine, there's nothing but thin air. If they manage to hit the mark, their reward is a few black hairs.

DID YOU KNOW?

SHORT-TAILED WEASEL:
A short-tailed weasel grasped in the talons of a hawk or owl can sometimes manage to squirm around, bite the neck of its assailant, and kill it.

♦ **SIZE AND COLOR:** 16 inches, including 4-inch tail; 6 to 8 ounces. Males 40 percent larger than females. White in winter except year-round black-tipped tail. Brown in summer with creamy white undersides.

♦ **REPRODUCTION:** Mate in July. Litter of 4 to 6 born in April. At birth, 1½ inches long and ⅒ ounce.

♦ **LIFE SPAN:** 5 to 6 years.
♦ **FOOD:** Mice, voles, lemmings, pikas, snowshoe hares, birds, insects, fish carcasses.
♦ **PREDATORS:** Minks, martens, red foxes, coyotes, goshawks, great horned owls, humans.
♦ **HABITAT AND RANGE:** Brushy or forested areas with broken terrain. Most of Alaska except islands.

SITKA BLACK-TAILED DEER

The Sitka black-tailed deer has a stockier build and shorter face than other types of blacktails, which in turn are more compact than the whitetails common in the Lower 48 states. A whitetail standing next to a Sitka black-tailed deer would look lean and long-legged. Sitka black-tailed deer have relatively small antlers, typically with 3 points on each side, including a 2- to 4-inch spike near the base of the antler called an eye guard. As with all members of the deer family except caribou, the females have no antlers.

Home for these Alaskan deer is the wet, coastal rain forest in a narrow strip of land between ocean and snowcapped coastal peaks. They are native to Southeast Alaska as far north as Juneau, but transplanting has extended their range to Kodiak Island and Prince William Sound.

Early each summer the receding snows permit these deer to move from the beach and spruce-hemlock forest below 1,500 feet elevation to alpine tundra up above timberline, where food is abundant. The alpine tundra is free of snow for only 3 to 5 months. Then the first heavy frosts of fall drive the deer down to lower elevations, where they feed on the leaves and young shoots of black currant and salmonberry found in alder slides and beneath the high timber.

The mating season begins in late October and peaks in

mid-November. Bucks lose weight throughout the rut, and by the end of December, they've used up most of their reserves of fat. Increasing snowfall drives the deer to even lower elevations.

Vegetation growing beneath the sheltering canopy of old-growth forest offers the deer food for the winter. But this is a lean time. The winter is even tougher for deer that find themselves in an extensively logged area. Snow accumulates twice as deep in a clear-cut area as in old-growth forest. Food is buried beneath the snow, and there are no trees to shelter the deer.

Heavy snow can drive the deer onto the beaches in search of food. They'll stay in the forest during high tide, then scrounge on the beaches at low tide for kelp and beach grass. But this diet offers little nutritional value. The deer can starve to death with full stomachs.

Spring brings respite. After the birth of fawns in May and June, the deer follow the receding snows back up the mountainsides. They eat skunk cabbage before its leaves uncurl, nibbling their way back up to the lush alpine country.

DID YOU KNOW?

SITKA BLACK-TAILED DEER:
Sitka black-tailed deer will move toward the bleating sound you can make by blowing on a long blade of grass held vertically in cupped hands.

♦ **SIZE AND COLOR:** 53 inches long; about 32 inches tall at shoulders; males average 120 pounds, females 80 pounds. Dark gray in winter, reddish brown in summer.

♦ **REPRODUCTION:** Mate in late October to late November, with 1 or 2 fawns born in May or June. Birth weight 6 to 8 pounds.

♦ **LIFE SPAN:** Average 6 years, but up to 12 years.

♦ **FOOD:** Skunk cabbage; blueberry and evergreen trailing blackberry bushes.

♦ **PREDATORS:** Wolves, coyotes, humans.

♦ **HABITAT AND RANGE:** Coastal rain forests; low elevations in winter, alpine meadows in summer. Kodiak Island, Prince William Sound, Southeast Alaska.

SNOWSHOE HARE

In Alaska and the Yukon, snowshoe hares give birth to the first of two or three yearly litters in mid-May. A typical litter has 4 young, called leverets, that nest near their birth site. During the day, the mother stays 50 to 100 feet away to avoid attracting predators to the nest.

Despite this precaution, two-thirds of all leverets perish within 2 weeks of birth, most falling victim to red squirrels. When a squirrel attacks, the mother rushes in, stomps her feet, clicks her teeth, and puts on a frightful show—but a determined squirrel usually prevails.

To offset these high mortality rates, hares are prolific breeders. Gestation lasts only about 36 days. Females mate again the same day their first litter of the year is born. The young are on their own a month after being born—just in time to make room for the next litter.

After the males' hormones kick in at the start of mating season, they become gymnastic, leaping and twisting in midair. They stand on their hind legs and box each other with their forepaws. Females box, too. Once they come into estrus, they shake their tails when they run.

To cope with predators, snowshoe hares have protruding eyes that offer almost 360-degree vision. Their 3½-inch-tall ears swivel independently. They're speedsters that leap, dodge, and twist to evade enemies. Their snowshoes—the 5-inch-long hind feet—spread their weight and provide great mobility. They're also camouflaged: white in winter, brown in summer, a mottled pattern between seasons.

Ultimately their own fecundity causes major population fluctuations. When food is abundant, they produce more young, and survival rates are higher. In response to this abundance of hares, the number of predators increases, especially lynx. At the same time, there's good evidence that the plants that hares forage respond to excessive browsing by increasing a chemical defense mechanism, giving the plants a bitter taste and reducing their digestibility.

This means less food for the hares at the same time that predator populations are at a peak. Soon predation and starvation combine to cause the hare population to plummet. Historically, the hares go through an 8- to 12-year boom-and-bust cycle (and the lynx population rises and falls with it).

DID YOU KNOW?

SHOWSHOE HARE:
Snowshoe hares don't have underground dens and tunnels, but instead stay in thick brush and natural depressions.

♦ **SIZE AND COLOR:** 18 to 20 inches long; 3 to 4 pounds. Brown in summer, white in winter, mottled between seasons.

♦ **REPRODUCTION:** Mate in mid-April, with first litter of 3 to 4 young born in mid-May. Second litter born 36 days later. Third litter some years. Birth weight 2 ounces.

♦ **LIFE SPAN:** 2 to 4 years.

♦ **FOOD:** Grasses plus leaves and buds of plants in summer; bark of aspen and willow trees in winter.

♦ **PREDATORS:** Lynx, foxes, martens, hawks, owls, humans; red squirrels prey on newborn hares.

♦ **HABITAT AND RANGE:** Wooded swamps, brushy areas, spruce forests. Throughout Alaska except Alaska Peninsula, lower Kuskokwim River Delta, and north of Brooks Range.

WOLF

Wolves are social animals, and the key to their survival is cooperative hunting. Going after large mammals is a dangerous business; an Alaskan moose can weigh 10 to 15 times as much as a wolf. Wolves sometimes end up with cracked ribs or fractured skulls from their attacks on prey.

Alaska's wolves have proven themselves to be versatile hunters in a variety of environments. They hunt caribou in the Arctic. They pursue mountain goats, and they go after Sitka black-tailed deer on the beaches of soggy Southeast Alaska.

Howling announces the presence of a wolf pack and warns intruders to not trespass. Instead of howling in one pitch, wolves harmonize. Three or four wolves harmonizing can give the impression of a dozen animals howling. When wolves disperse to hunt and roam, howling helps them locate other members of the pack. And there's a definite increase in howling during the late winter months when wolves mate. Some observers think howling is prompted by restlessness and anxiety. Others point to the obvious: it's fun.

A typical wolf pack has 6 to 12 animals, although packs may get as large as 30 wolves. One male wolf (the alpha male) dominates other males in a pack, while an alpha female dominates the other female wolves. As a general rule, only the alpha male and alpha female mate. Alpha females sometimes lead the pack. And they always decide where to den—an important responsibility because the site of the den determines where the pack will hunt for 5 or 6 weeks.

A wolf can consume one-fifth its body weight at a sitting. After eating its fill, a wolf may bury leftovers, just as a dog buries bones. When wolves return from a hunt, pups will nip at the corners of an adult's mouth, prompting the adult to regurgitate food for them. Wolf pups also raise a paw to solicit food. Since domestic dogs are descendants of wolves, we shouldn't be surprised that it's so easy to train a pet dog to shake hands.

Both adult wolves and pups "play fight." They bow to signal the start of play. Sometimes they bounce, look away momentarily, and then peer over their shoulder at the intended playmate. They "grin" by pulling their lips back. When a wolf wants affection, it uses its snout to bunt another wolf on the chin. Your dog can't reach your chin, so it bunts your hand.

DID YOU KNOW?

WOLF:
The territories of wolf packs in Alaska range in size from 300 to 1,000 square miles, with the average territory being 600 square miles.

◆ **SIZE AND COLOR:** Males 5 to 6½ feet long, including 14- to 19-inch tail; 40 to 150 pounds (average range 80 to 115). Females about 10 percent smaller. Gray and black most common, but ranges from black to white.

◆ **REPRODUCTION:** Mate in February and March. Litter, average 5 pups, born in May and early June. Birth weight less than 1 pound.

◆ **LIFE SPAN:** 10 years.

◆ **FOOD:** Moose, caribou, Dall sheep, mountain goats, deer, small mammals.

◆ **PREDATORS:** Other wolves, humans.

◆ **HABITAT AND RANGE:** Varied, including arctic tundra, brushy areas, rain forests. All of mainland Alaska, Unimak Island in the Aleutians, and major islands of Southeast Alaska except for Admiralty, Baranof, and Chichagof.

WOLVERINE

Wolverines look like stout little bears. They're 30 pounds of muscle, claws, jaws, and teeth, with astonishing strength and endurance. Naturalists in Denali National Park and Preserve saw a wolverine drag a dead Dall sheep that weighed over 120 pounds for 2 miles down a mountain, across a shallow, fast-moving river, and up a steep bank. Wolverines pursued by snowmobiles have loped 40 miles through deep snow without stopping. Despite the physical resemblance to bears, the wolverine is actually the largest land-dwelling member of the weasel family.

Even on a routine day, a wolverine may walk 10 to 30 miles, from rivers to mountaintops, while hunting and scavenging in its 100- to 300-square-mile territory.

Although wolverines successfully prey on snowshoe hares, and other small mammals and birds, they are too small and slow to be efficient predators of larger prey. Instead, wolverines evolved to be supreme scavengers; some biologists call them the hyenas of the North. One study found that in winter, wolverines in the Brooks Range live almost entirely on carrion, most often caribou. With their powerful jaws and strong teeth, they eat everything, including hide, hooves, and bone.

Wolverines live a feast-or-famine life, so they consume prodigious quantities of food when it's available. The wolverine's scientific name (*Gulo gulo*) means "glutton." If there's too much food to eat at once, wolverines spray the remains with a vile-smelling musk, then cache it for future use.

The wolverine will occasionally break into an unoccupied cabin and make a smelly mess of the inside. Such behavior has prompted some people to call wolverines "devil bears," but it's hunger that leads them in the door and habit that dictates leaving the musky aroma.

Alaskan Natives and settlers have long favored wolverine fur to trim the hoods of winter parkas. Wolverine hairs have a tapered shape that sheds frost and moisture well, and the hair doesn't break or pull out, even after years of use.

According to the lore of trappers and hunters, the wolverine is vicious and unusually aggressive. Tales abound of wolverines driving grizzly bears and wolves away from carcasses. Some stories may be exaggerated, but there's no question a wolverine is well equipped for combat and has strength out of proportion to its size.

DID YOU KNOW?

WOLVERINE:
In northern Alaska and the Interior, most young wolverines (called kits) are born in snow tunnels that are up to 60 yards long.

✦ **SIZE AND COLOR:** 36 to 44 inches long, including 15- to 18-inch tail; average 25 to 35 pounds (50 maximum). Dark to golden brown; two creamy white to light-brown stripes start on shoulders and join at base of tail.

✦ **REPRODUCTION:** Mate in May through July, with 2 to 4 young born in January, February, or March. Birth weight less than 1 pound.

✦ **LIFE SPAN:** 8 to 10 years.
✦ **FOOD:** Omnivorous; almost anything, including carrion.
✦ **PREDATORS:** Wolves, humans.
✦ **HABITAT AND RANGE:** Most common in forested and alpine habitats, but in almost all habitats seasonally, from mountainous areas to lowlands. All of Alaska except for some islands, but most common in the Interior.

Male walrus sleep in the sun on the rocky shoreline of Round Island, a state wildlife sanctuary.

MARINE MAMMALS

BELUGA WHALE

Imagine seeing a whale, a white whale, in a freshwater river. Belugas (the word *belukha* is Russian for "white") often feed on salmon near estuaries, and sometimes they follow the salmon far upstream. In the summer of 1993, people saw four belugas near Fort Yukon, 800 miles up the Yukon River. Most belugas remain in shallow water during the summer, favoring coastal areas with bays, coves, and estuaries.

Like dolphins and killer whales, belugas are gregarious. They usually travel in pods of 2 to 10 adults and juveniles, though pods of up to 100 animals are fairly common.

Belugas have a short "beak" that houses 40 to 44 teeth. They grab their prey and swallow it whole. Belugas feed at a variety of depths, from shallow water to more than 500 feet down. They hunt and travel in murky water by using echolocation, bouncing sound waves off objects. Along with dolphins and killer whales, belugas have one of the most sensitive sonar systems of any marine mammal.

When scientists first recorded the vocalizations of belugas in 1949, they said the whales sounded like an orchestra tuning up. Belugas whistle, shriek, and make a variety of birdlike calls. Nineteenth-century whalers called belugas "sea canaries." Researchers still haven't deciphered the language of belugas, but coordinated herd movements when belugas are hunting or being hunted suggest that these mammals understand one another.

During winter, many of Alaska's belugas live amidst the pack ice of the Bering Sea. Echolocation guides them through ice-clogged waterways. They maneuver in tight spots by paddling their flippers; they can even swim backward and upside down. They don't have a dorsal fin; it would hinder movement through the ice. A 2- to 4-inch layer of blubber insulates them from frigid arctic water, and their white color serves as camouflage.

Belugas typically travel 2 to 5 miles per hour, with a top speed, in short bursts, of a little over 14 miles per hour. That's not fast enough to flee killer whales. To escape, belugas will hide along an underwater bank where their pursuers' sonar sounds become scrambled.

Alaskan Natives still harvest belugas, although it's difficult to catch a beluga off guard. When resting, one side of a beluga's brain remains alert while the other side relaxes. One watchful eye is always open.

DID YOU KNOW?

BELUGA WHALE:
Belugas shed their skin each summer by rubbing it on gravel or coarse sand bottoms. Pre-molt belugas are yellowish and scarred, but after molting, they're shiny white.

◆ **SIZE AND COLOR:** Males average 13 feet and 3,300 pounds; females 12 feet and 3,000 pounds. Dark gray at birth, blue gray as juveniles, white as adults.

◆ **REPRODUCTION:** Mate in spring. Gestation of 14 months, with single calf born from May to July every other year. At birth, 5 feet and 70 pounds.

◆ **LIFE SPAN:** 35 to 40 years.

◆ **FOOD:** Over 100 sea-life species, including crabs, clams, fish, squid.

◆ **PREDATORS:** Transient killer whales, polar bears, humans.

◆ **HABITAT AND RANGE:** Coastal waters and estuaries in summer; pack ice in winter. North and west coast of Alaska, south into Bristol Bay. Isolated population of 600 to 1,100 in Cook Inlet.

BOWHEAD WHALE

The bowhead whale's cavernous mouth opens wide enough to engulf a standing polar bear—but its throat is only a bit over 4 inches in diameter. That's big enough, however, to swallow the small shrimplike crustaceans known as krill that are the mainstay of the bowhead's diet.

Bowheads strain krill through huge plates of the horny material called baleen, found instead of teeth in the mouths of baleen whales. Bowheads have anywhere from 460 to 720 dark-gray baleen plates that are the longest of any whale—an average of 10 to 12 feet. To accommodate the plates, the bowhead has a huge head that is one-third of its overall length. The bowhead's name derives from the shape of its jaw, which curves strongly and resembles an archer's bow.

Some 7,500 bowheads winter in pack ice of the Bering Sea. In spring, they head north through the Bering Strait, then travel east to summer feeding grounds at Banks Island, Canada. During this spring migration, they travel alone or in groups of 2 or 3, moving at a steady 4 knots.

Although bowheads can smash through ice 1 to 2 feet thick to create breathing holes, heavy pack ice occasionally blocks their passage, producing memorable concentrations of whales. From a plane, a biologist once counted 332 bowheads in an open area of sea within the pack ice that was only

15 miles long and less than a mile wide. During their fall migration back to the Bering Sea, bowheads commonly travel in groups of up to 50. Migrating bowheads feed sparingly and vocalize frequently.

Eskimos have utilized bowheads for centuries. Bones were used to shoe the runners of sleds. Jawbones and ribs were used in home construction. Whale gut was made into waterproof clothing. Sleds, cups, buckets, and dishes were fashioned from baleen. And, of course, bowheads provided food.

Commercial whalers called bowheads the "right whale" (not to be confused with Atlantic and Pacific right whales), because it swam slowly, floated when harpooned, and yielded 100 barrels of oil. From a single bowhead, whalers also could get 1,500 pounds of baleen, used in making skirt hoops, corset stays, buggy whips, and umbrella ribs. Between 1850 and 1906, commercial whaling reduced the bowhead population to less than 3,000. The invention of spring steel in 1906 saved the bowhead.

DID YOU KNOW?

BOWHEAD WHALE:
Bowhead whales sing in a voice that covers 7 octaves.

◆ SIZE AND COLOR: 50 to 60 feet long; up to 70 tons. Silky black, with white or cream-color patch on chin. Some bowheads have a gray stripe around tail stock.
◆ REPRODUCTION: Single calf born in April, May, or early June after 13-month gestation. At birth, 13 to 15 feet long and 1 ton.
◆ LIFE SPAN: Average may be 50 to 60 years, but little is known. In bowheads harvested recently by Natives, researchers have found harpoon tips made of ivory and steel that date to 1900 or earlier.
◆ FOOD: Mainly krill.
◆ PREDATORS: Transient killer whales, humans.
◆ HABITAT AND RANGE: Near and in pack ice year-round. Chukchi and Beaufort seas in summer; Bering Sea in winter.

DALL PORPOISE

Dall porpoises are fast swimmers, probably the fastest mammals in the sea. They've been clocked at 30 miles per hour. These porpoises frequently put their speed to use in a manner that makes them one of Alaska's most visible and popular marine mammals: they're bow riders. They enjoy riding the bow wave from boats of all sizes and have been known to accompany boats for ½ hour or more.

Seen from the deck of a boat, the Dall porpoise's bold black-and-white coloration is striking. Most of its body is a shiny jet black, which sets off the white tip of its triangular dorsal fin and the white trailing edge of its tail. From above, you can see a bright white patch on its sides. This white patch actually extends down from the sides and across the belly, covering the middle third of the porpoise's body.

Dall porpoises don't leap clear out of the water like dolphins, but most of them do kick up a rooster tail when they surface to breathe. The rooster tail isn't caused by the porpoise's tail, however; it results from water coming off its head as the porpoise breaks the surface.

These porpoises are sometimes mistaken for killer whales. They share similar black-and-white markings, but the Dall porpoise is much smaller and lacks the killer whale's prominent dorsal fin. Dall porpoises and harbor porpoises are similar in size and shape, so color is the key to telling these two species apart. Harbor porpoises are a subdued gray and brown.

Dall porpoises commonly travel in groups of 2 to 20, although feeding aggregations of 200 have been seen in Alaskan waters. The largest group ever recorded numbered 3,000 and was spotted by a National Marine Mammals Laboratory scientist near Stephens Passage in Southeast Alaska.

The most important food for the Dall porpoise in Alaska is squid. The porpoise also preys on relatively small schooling fish such as herring, hake, capelin, and jack mackerel. It tends to be a bottom feeder and is capable of diving as deep as 10,000 feet.

Only humans and transient killer whales prey on the Dall porpoise. It's just too fast for most predators. This porpoise has a chunky, muscular body that tapers abruptly at the head and tail. Seen from the side, it roughly resembles a thick log with each end cut at a 45-degree angle.

The Makah Indians of Washington State called the Dall porpoise "broken tail" because of a "hump" on its tail, a large mass of muscle that's believed to boost its swimming speed.

DID YOU KNOW?

DALL PORPOISE:
The Dall porpoise (like Dall sheep) is named after American zoologist William Dall, who traveled in Alaska during the 1870s and was the first naturalist to document the species.

◆ **SIZE AND COLOR:** 6 feet long; 300 pounds. Black body with boldly marked white belly and flanks, white-tipped dorsal fin, white-tipped tail.
◆ **REPRODUCTION:** Single calf born after 11- to 12-month gestation. At birth, 3 feet long and 85 pounds.
◆ **LIFE SPAN:** 20 years.

◆ **FOOD:** Squid, schooling fish.
◆ **PREDATORS:** Transient killer whales, humans.
◆ **HABITAT AND RANGE:** Coastal and offshore waters. Common in Gulf of Alaska and Bering Sea in spring and summer; coastal areas as far south as Baja California in fall and winter.

GRAY WHALE

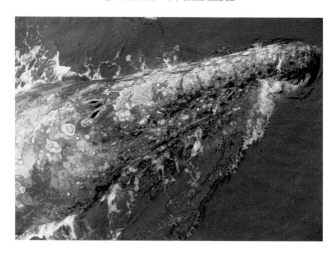

Gray whales have a unique feeding technique. They lie on the ocean floor, turn on their right side, and suck in mouthfuls of muck and sediment. Pressure from their tongue strains water, mud, and silt through dozens of creamy yellow baleen plates in their mouth; small crustaceans called amphipods, which look like sand fleas, are trapped in coarse hair along the trailing edge of the baleen and become the whale's food.

For reasons that are not understood, almost all gray whales feed only on their right side. The 18-inch-long horny plates of baleen on the right side wear away with age. The whales often have a multitude of scars and scratches on the right side of the head.

Gray whales spend the winter in their breeding grounds along Mexico's Baja California coast and the summer in the rich feeding grounds of the Bering and Chukchi seas off Alaska. They consume enough food during the summer months in Alaska to sustain them during their migration to Baja. A combination of cold weather, diminishing food, and the need for pregnant females to give birth in warmer waters drives them south. They don't eat during their lengthy journey to Baja or on the return trip in the spring.

Pregnant females are the first gray whales to begin migrating south from Alaska, leaving in October. Beginning in

November, all the grays are on their way to Baja, swimming at a steady 5 knots. They travel about 100 miles a day, arriving in late December after a migration that is the longest of any marine mammal's. In the warm, shallow coves and lagoons off the coast of Baja, they mate.

Gestation takes about a year, so some females are giving birth while others are mating. Females with newborn calves avoid the mating activity by sticking to the edges of the lagoons. Female grays are dedicated mothers, defending their calves aggressively against attacks by sharks.

Female gray whales have rich milk—over 50 percent fat—and the calves double in length, reaching some 30 feet, by the time the gray whales set off on their spring migration northward. Most of the whales migrate all the way to northern Alaska and the Chukchi Sea, but a few stop and spend the summer between Northern California and Southeast Alaska.

Gray whales were nearly hunted to extinction by the 1920s. But the species has recovered and now numbers about 20,000—enough that, while still protected, gray whales have been removed from the Endangered Species List.

DID YOU KNOW?

GRAY WHALE:
Gray whales share an odd habit with killer whales: they like to scratch themselves on selected sandbars and gravel beaches.

◆ **SIZE AND COLOR:** Males average 39 feet long, females 42 feet; average weight 35 tons. Mottled gray, with lots of barnacles and yellow, white, and orange patches.

◆ **REPRODUCTION:** Mate in winter. Single calf born from January to March after 1-year gestation. At birth, 12 to 16 feet long and 1,200 to 1,500 pounds.

◆ **LIFE SPAN:** 40 to 69 years.

◆ **FOOD:** Small crustaceans, tube worms, opossum shrimp.

◆ **PREDATORS:** Transient killer whales, humans; sharks prey on calves.

◆ **HABITAT AND RANGE:** Coastal waters. Bering and Chukchi seas in summer; Baja California in winter.

HARBOR SEAL

Harbor seals are solitary in water, but tend to be gregarious on land. Groups numbering in the hundreds are common in some areas. A single seal on land has to spend more time watching for predators than the individuals in a group do. Seals in a group can get more rest.

After harbor seals haul out onto land, they rub, scratch, yawn, sleep, and periodically glance around for predators. The harbor seal often rests on land or ice in a banana-shaped position that looks uncomfortable.

Harbor seals are slow and clumsy on land. Unlike sea lions, harbor seals can't rotate their hind flippers forward to help them walk, nor can they lift their belly off the ground. They steer and brake with their front flippers and just drag their rear flippers behind them. They wiggle and hump along like portly caterpillars.

Harbor seals are much more at home in the water. When you see one beneath your kayak, it looks sleek and graceful. An inquisitive seal will often quietly surface near a small craft, look 90 degrees in each direction, then drop vertically into the depths. Poof. Gone.

Harbor seals are usually found in shallow coastal waters and estuaries. They often ascend rivers to feed on fish that travel upstream on the high tide; the seals then haul out at low tide to sleep until the next high tide. In spring, they may follow fish hundreds of miles upriver.

Harbor seals can dive to depths of more than 400 feet and stay down for almost ½ hour, although they usually submerge for only 5 to 6 minutes. When they dive, their heart rate drops from 85 beats a minute to 15. Blood flow becomes concentrated in the body core, keeping their temperature at 100 degrees Fahrenheit to protect heart, lungs, and other vital organs. Most harbor seals in southern Alaska are born on land. But in some places—such as Glacier Bay and parts of Prince William Sound—seals have their pups on ice floes in glacier-fed waters which offer protection from bears and other terrestrial predators. In addition, killer whales don't usually hunt in these murky, silty, glacial waters.

A large number of pups are sometimes concentrated in a few acres of water and ice, but a mother returning from hunting can recognize her own pup by its voice. Seal milk has 10 times the fat content of cow's milk, so seal pups grow quickly. Pups double in size within a month of birth.

DID YOU KNOW?

HARBOR SEAL:
There is a year-round freshwater colony of harbor seals at Alaska's Lake Iliamna.

♦ **SIZE AND COLOR:** 6 feet long; 250 pounds. Black to almost white, with variable-colored rings, spots, blotches.

♦ **REPRODUCTION:** Mate in July and August. Single pup born in the following May or June. At birth, 3 feet long and 25 pounds.

♦ **LIFE SPAN:** 30 years.

♦ **FOOD:** Shrimp, squid, octopus, capelin, pollock, sand lance, herring, smelt, cod, salmon.

♦ **PREDATORS:** Transient killer whales, sea lions, bears, humans; bald eagles take pups.

♦ **HABITAT AND RANGE:** Coastal waters and rivers. Southeast, Southcentral, and Southwest Alaska; Western Alaska only as far north as the Kuskokwim Bay/Bethel area.

HUMPBACK WHALE

Humpback whales migrate each spring from Hawaii or Mexico to the rich feeding grounds of Alaska. During this migration, they segregate themselves by age, sex, and reproductive status. Immature whales and newly pregnant females head north first. They're followed by mature males and by females that have just started lactating, with their calves.

The whales usually travel in pods of 2 to 5 animals at a leisurely pace of 2 to 4 knots. Calves nurse during the migration, but the other humpbacks eat nothing during their 80-day journey to Alaska or on the trip back south in the fall.

Some humpbacks return to the same area of Alaska each summer. One researcher saw the same whale return to Glacier Bay for 12 years in a row. And a few humpbacks reside in Alaska year-round. You can recognize individual whales by their flukes, which are unique in color and shape.

The humpback whale belongs to the genus *Megaptera*, which means "big winged," an apt description of its 12- to 15-foot-long flippers, which flare out like wings when the animal heaves itself out of the water. Female humpbacks caress their calves with their flippers.

Humpbacks are especially known for their singing, a sound that can be heard underwater for 5 miles by humans. Whales hear the main song from 19 miles away, and low tones carry

115 miles. Only the male humpbacks sing. Most of the singing occurs during the winter mating season in Hawaii or Mexico, although humpbacks also sing while migrating.

Once the whales arrive in Alaska, most singing stops and intensive feeding begins. The humpback employs a variety of feeding techniques. If food is concentrated near the surface, the whale "lunge feeds" by opening its mouth wide and plowing into the midst of the prey: schools of small fish or the small shrimplike crustaceans known as krill. The humpback also rolls on its side to feed laterally, "flick feeding" by using its flukes to concentrate and stun food.

One or more humpbacks will consciously create a "bubble net" by exhaling underwater and sending up a ring of grapefruit-size bubbles to confuse and trap prey. The whales then swim up inside the ring of bubbles with mouth agape. Instead of teeth, the upper jaw of the humpback contains long plates of the material called baleen. A feeding humpback takes in about 500 gallons of water at a time and then filters the water through these baleen plates, trapping as much as 100 pounds of krill and other food.

DID YOU KNOW?

HUMPBACK WHALE: A humpback whale consumes as much as 2 tons of food per day during its summer stay in Alaska, giving it a 3- to 4-inch-thick layer of blubber for the fall migration.

◆ **SIZE AND COLOR:** Males average 46 feet and 25 tons; females 49 feet and 35 tons. Black body with some white on belly and throat.

◆ **REPRODUCTION:** Single calf born in February after 11½-month gestation. Size at birth 12 feet and 2 tons.

◆ **LIFE SPAN:** 50 years.

◆ **FOOD:** Krill; some herring, capelin, sand lance, other small fish.

◆ **PREDATORS:** Transient killer whales, humans.

◆ **HABITAT AND RANGE:** Close to shore in coastal waters. Bering Strait and Chukchi Sea to Southeast Alaska in summer; Hawaii and Mexico in winter.

KILLER WHALE

Researchers in Canadian coastal waters first began taking identification photos of killer whales in 1970 when they realized that the scars, scratches, and nicks on each whale's dorsal fin—combined with a distinctive gray or white saddle behind the fin—could serve to identify individual animals. Male killer-whale dorsal fins are tall (up to 6 feet) and straight; females fins are shorter and curved.

By 1975 researchers recognized that, year after year, the same whales usually traveled with the same companions. They found that killer whales—also known as orcas, from their scientific name *Orcinus orca*—lived in groups of either resident pods (which stay in the same area through much of the year) or transient pods (which roam widely).

Resident pods are matriarchal societies, and since females live as long as 70 years, a pod often includes several generations of whales. These pods range in size from 5 to 40 animals. Resident pods feed on fish such as squid, salmon, cod, and halibut.

The family makeup of transient pods is not well known, but the transients do have different feeding habits. In fact, it's now apparent that the transient pods are what gave these whales their fearsome reputation. The transient pods travel far, often covering a 500- to 900-mile section of coastline. They are supreme hunters, preying on marine mammals, including

Steller sea lions, seals, sea otters, and gray whales and other large whales. They've been known to flip 180-pound harbor seals in the air, toying with them just as a house cat toys with a mouse.

Both transient and resident killer whales hunt communally, swim at speeds up to at least 28 miles per hour, and have 40 to 56 conical, interlocking teeth that curve back toward the throat. Contrary to popular belief, the teeth are not razor-sharp; each tooth is the size of a human thumb, and about as sharp.

All killer whales are vocal animals that communicate with clicks, whistles, and pulsed calls. But each pod apparently has its own dialect, and the sounds of whales in resident pods differ from those of transient whales.

The transients and residents also differ in other ways. The tip of a resident killer whale's dorsal fin is rounded, whereas a transient's is pointed. Resident pods stay together for years, while transient pods often change members. Transients apparently don't breed with residents, and some biologists think the transients constitute a separate subspecies.

DID YOU KNOW?

KILLER WHALE:
Resting pods of killer whales breathe in unison (through blowholes the size of a human fist) and, when traveling, often dive in unison.

◆ **SIZE AND COLOR:** Males reach 32 feet long; 6-foot-tall dorsal fin; 9 to 10 tons. Females to 28 feet; 3-foot-tall dorsal fin; 5 to 6 tons. Black body; white belly, chin, eye patch; gray or white saddle behind dorsal fin.

◆ **REPRODUCTION:** It's believed that mating occurs year-round. Single calf born after gestation of 13 to 16 months. At birth, 8 feet and 400 pounds.

◆ **LIFE SPAN:** Males 30 to 50 years, females 50 to 70.

◆ **FOOD:** Salmon, cod, halibut, herring, seals, sea otters, birds, Steller sea lions, other whales.

◆ **PREDATORS:** Humans.

◆ **HABITAT AND RANGE:** Coastal waters along continental shelf. Entire coast of Alaska, except where pack ice excludes them because of their dorsal fin.

NORTHERN FUR SEAL

Except for the 3 to 4 months a year when northern fur seals haul out to mate on the Pribilof Islands in the Bering Sea, they live in the open ocean. They sleep at sea in what old-time seal hunters called a jug-handle position. Just picture a shrimp sleeping on its back. The seal floats with its tail and both rear flippers curled back toward its head. It grasps one front flipper with its rear flippers and lifts its head and nose out of the water.

Northern fur seals have long rear flippers that are hairless and laced with blood vessels. On warm days, they wave the flippers in the air to help dissipate body heat. Overheating can be a problem for these seals because they're wrapped in blubber and covered with warm fur. Humans have always prized this fur. Hunters harvested an estimated 600,000 northern fur seals between 1899 and 1909. The population dipped as low as 200,000 to 300,000 before protective measures were enacted. Today there are about 1.3 million northern fur seals.

These seals feed at night when prey species rise toward the surface. The seals commonly dive to depths of 66 feet and stay underwater for 1 minute, but they are capable of diving to more than 600 feet and of staying down for more than 5 minutes. Fish and squid up to 10 inches long can be swallowed whole underwater. The seals bring anything bigger to the surface, where they tear it apart with hard shakes of the head.

Their diet varies with location as they travel the coast of North America between Alaska and California. Off the coast of Washington, they favor salmon and rockfish. In Alaska, squid and herring are preferred.

Male northern fur seals begin coming ashore in the Pribilof Islands in mid-May to establish breeding territories. A male will stake a claim to a stretch of beach and defend it against other males. Each breeding male has a harem of about 40 to 50 females, and these males reign supreme for 2 years before being replaced by more vigorous males.

Pregnant females reach the Pribilofs in mid-June, and each gives birth to a single pup within 2 days of arrival. Ten days after the pup is born, the female mates again. Then she begins making foraging trips to sea. When a mother returns from a trip, she locates her pup from among hundreds of identical-looking pups by its voice and smell. Mothers nurse for a day or two, then forage at sea for 8 to 10 days. Despite this intermittent feeding pattern, the pups double in size by autumn. By November, all the northern fur seals have returned to sea.

DID YOU KNOW?

NORTHERN FUR SEAL:
Male northern fur seals that are breeding don't eat during the 2-month mating season, and they lose 20 percent of their body weight.

◆ **SIZE AND COLOR:** Males 6½ feet long; 300 to 600 pounds. Females a little over 4 feet long; 65 to 110 pounds. Silvery gray to brown; pups black at birth.

◆ **REPRODUCTION:** Mate in late June and July. Single pup born after gestation of 11 to 12 months. At birth, 2 feet long and 11 to 12 pounds.

◆ **LIFE SPAN:** 26 years.

◆ **FOOD:** Pollock, herring, capelin, squid.

◆ **PREDATORS:** Transient killer whales, Steller sea lions, sharks, humans.

◆ **HABITAT AND RANGE:** Ashore on the Pribilof Islands during summer. On the open sea 7 to 10 months a year offshore from Southeast Alaska to California.

POLAR BEAR

B iologists theorize that 100,000 years ago a population of brown/grizzly bears became isolated in Siberia and, with remarkable quickness, evolved into polar bears. Where brown/grizzly bears have a broad head and burly chest, polar bears have a narrow head, long neck, and hindquarters that are wider and higher than the front part of their body. Polar bears thus have a wedge shape that enhances their ability to slice through the water.

Scientists classify the polar bear as a marine mammal. Its Latin name, *Ursus maritimus*, means "sea bear." With their partially webbed feet, polar bears are powerful swimmers. They dog-paddle 6½ miles an hour, dive to depths of 30 feet, and stay down for more than a minute.

A polar bear's fur loses 90 percent of its insulation value when wet. A thick layer of blubber, not fur, keeps polar bears warm in the water. They're so well insulated that they overheat easily. Their normal temperature is 98.6 degrees Fahrenheit, just like humans. The temperature of a bear walking a little over 4 miles per hour quickly soars to 100 degrees—feverish.

The bear's body combats this problem by shunting blood to extremities that don't retain heat well: nose, legs, and footpads. The bear rolls onto its back and sticks its legs and feet into the air. And if there's water nearby, the bear jumps in.

Alaska's polar bears, numbering between 3,000 and 5,000, occupy two fairly distinct areas. One segment lives east of Point Barrow (Alaska's northernmost point) and has a range that extends into Canada. The other polar bears live west of Point Barrow and all the way to Russia. The animals spend most of their lives along the edges of the drifting, ever-changing pack ice that recedes from Alaska's northern coast in spring and summer and returns in autumn. On Halloween night in Barrow, the children who go trick-or-treating are accompanied by armed patrols watching for polar bears.

Pregnant females den either on the heavy pack ice or on land such as the coastal plain of the Arctic National Wildlife Refuge in far northeast Alaska. The overall engineering of a polar bear den is similar to an igloo. During winter, bears may wander as far as 70 miles inland, but they rarely linger because food is scarce. They return to the pack ice to hunt ringed seals, the staple of the polar bear's diet.

DID YOU KNOW?

POLAR BEAR:
The bottom of a polar bear's foot is thickly furred, which muffles sound that might otherwise be transmitted through the ice to prey below.

♦ **SIZE AND COLOR:** Males 8½ feet long; 4 feet tall at shoulders; average 900 pounds (up to 1,400 pounds). Females 6½ feet long; 500 pounds. White with a yellowish tinge.

♦ **REPRODUCTION:** Mate in late March to May, with 1 to 3 cubs (usually twins) born in December or January. At birth, 10 inches long and 1 to 2 pounds.

♦ **LIFE SPAN:** 25 to 30 years.

♦ **FOOD:** Ringed seals, carrion, bearded seals, beluga whales, walrus, eggs, kelp.

♦ **PREDATORS:** Transient killer whales, humans; wolves and male polar bears prey on cubs.

♦ **HABITAT AND RANGE:** North on pack ice to latitude 75 degrees; south on pack ice to St. Matthew and Nunivak islands. Alaska's northern and northwest coast in winter.

RINGED SEAL

The ringed seal is an arctic animal that spends its days both on and beneath the ice. These seals have long, sturdy claws on their front flippers for digging cone-shaped breathing holes up from the water and through to the surface of the ice. They start a hole when the ice is thin and maintain it even after the ice has become more than 6 feet thick.

A ringed seal builds a denning lair, a sort of snow cave, on top of the ice. A typical lair is about 6 feet wide and 9 feet long, and pups are born and raised there. Pups arrive with a fine, white, woolly coat called lanugo that they begin shedding after 2 to 3 weeks. By the age of 6 to 8 weeks, pups are silver-colored on the belly and dark gray on top. The characteristic rings and spots of the ringed seal grow in as they mature.

Adult ringed seals lose weight during the spring and early summer because they don't feed much when they're breeding, nursing, and molting. The seals start giving birth in March and don't finish molting until July. Their weight drops 20 to 30 percent during this time. But with renewed feeding, they grow quite portly by fall. Typically, a ringed seal's girth is 80 percent of its length, and half its body weight is hide and blubber.

Ringed seals feed at two levels in the arctic marine food chain. They eat small fish, especially those in the cod family. And they eat zooplankton that the fish feed on. They sometimes eat the same sorts of krill that bowhead whales consume, and in fact may compete with bowheads for food.

Ringed seals are the principal prey of polar bears, which wait on the ice to grab the seals when they swim up to their breathing hole to surface. Polar bears will also crash through the roof of a denning lair to catch the seals inside.

Ringed seals are an important source of food for other arctic animals as well. During the winter, arctic foxes follow polar bears and scavenge blubber and scraps from the bear's seal kills. In spring, 45 percent of all ringed seal pups in some areas are killed by arctic foxes. Ravens and glaucous gulls can get pups when lairs disintegrate during mild temperatures. Wolves and wolverines occasionally locate lairs by scent and dig out the pups.

This predation has made ringed seals wary. One study found that after ringed seals haul out onto the ice, they rest an average of 26 seconds and then look around for 7 seconds, and then continue repeating this cycle.

DID YOU KNOW?

RINGED SEAL:
When ringed seal pups are only a few days old, they can dive 60 feet or more beneath the surface of the sea.

◆ **SIZE AND COLOR:** 4 feet long; 140 to 180 pounds. Variable: usually gray back with black spots ringed by white marks; lighter colored belly.

◆ **REPRODUCTION:** Mate in April to May. Single pup born after gestation of about 11 months. Birth weight 7 to 10 pounds.

◆ **LIFE SPAN:** 25 to 35 years.

◆ **FOOD:** Arctic cod, small fish, shrimp, small crustaceans (krill and amphipods).

◆ **PREDATORS:** Polar bears, humans; arctic foxes and occasional other animals prey on pups.

◆ **HABITAT AND RANGE:** Close to shore on shore-fast ice in winter; on pack ice in summer. Northern and western Alaska as far south as Nunivak Island. Move seasonally with the pack ice.

SEA OTTER

Sea otters have prodigious appetites. A study in Orca Inlet near Prince William Sound found that adult sea otters were each consuming 14 Dungeness crabs a day, eating an amount equal to 20 to 25 percent of their body weight daily. The otters usually dive to depths of 60 feet or less and stay down for a minute or two. After they surface with their food, they rest it on their chest as they eat.

A sea otter will sometimes bring up a rock held in a loose flap of skin, rest the rock on its chest, and crack clams or mussels against it. You can see the otter turn its head aside and close its eyes at the moment of impact. Sea otters spend about one-third of their day diving and eating.

Pregnant sea otters usually give birth in late spring or early summer, although pups can be born any time of year. Alaska's sea otters occasionally give birth on shore; California's sea otters always give birth in the water. Mothers commonly float on their back so the pups can preen, sleep, and travel while resting on her chest. Sea otter pups face the threat of predators. Near Amchitka Island in the Aleutians, bald eagles have been seen snatching pups while their mothers are diving for food. When sea otters come ashore around Prince William Sound, coyotes take pups.

Sea otters are descendants of river otters, but they're larger and are never seen in freshwater rivers or lakes. A sea otter spends a good bit of time each day grooming its luxurious fur. The sea otter's underfur varies in density from 170,000 hairs per square inch on its feet to 1 million per square inch on its forelegs (by comparison, a dog has 1,000 to 6,000 hairs per square inch).

Sea otters don't have blubber; a layer of air trapped in the fur keeps their skin dry and insulates them from cold water. Dirty, oily fur allows water to penetrate to an otter's skin, bringing hypothermia and death. So the otters twist and roll and dive after eating, in order to clean their fur. Otters get air into their fur by floating belly down, blowing bubbles, and rubbing them into the fur.

To a human observer, all this rolling, diving, and splashing may look like play, but to an otter, it's serious business. Nonetheless, sea otters are a joy to watch. As they sleep on the water, sea otters often hold hands so they don't float away from each other. Otters will also wrap kelp around themselves so they won't get washed into shore.

DID YOU KNOW?

SEA OTTER:
Sea otters are able to detect and avoid the dangerous toxins in clams and mussels that cause paralytic shellfish poisoning in humans.

◆ **SIZE AND COLOR:** Males 5 feet and 70 pounds; females 4 feet and 60 pounds. Dark brown with lighter head that turns grayish white with age.
◆ **REPRODUCTION:** Peak mating season from September to October. Single pup, commonly born in May. At birth, 10 inches and 5 pounds.
◆ **LIFE SPAN:** Males 10 to 15 years, females 15 to 20.

◆ **FOOD:** Crabs, clams, mussels, fish, urchins.
◆ **PREDATORS:** Transient killer whales, humans; bald eagles and coyotes prey on pups.
◆ **HABITAT AND RANGE:** Shallow coastal waters, especially kelp beds. From Southeast Alaska to Prince William Sound to the Aleutian Islands.

STELLER SEA LION

S teller sea lions are found from northwestern California to Japan along the North Pacific Rim, but most of the world's population lives in Alaska—70 percent, according to a 1989 survey.

Although the population is stable in Southeast Alaska, it has declined sharply over much of the sea lion's range. In 1950, a total of 105,000 Steller sea lions was counted at major rookeries and haul-outs between the Kenai Peninsula and the Aleutian Islands. By 1989, the count in that area had dropped to 23,000. In 1990, the Steller sea lion was classified as a threatened species under the Endangered Species Act.

Reasons for the decline are uncertain. A combination of factors—disease, changes in environmental conditions, conflicts with commercial fishermen—could be involved. Studies in the Gulf of Alaska showed that about half the sea lion's diet was pollock. Sea lions consumed more pollock in the 1980s than in the 1970s, but the pollock they caught in the '80s were smaller—so the sea lions had to spend more time and energy to get the same amount of food. The body size of Steller sea lions near Kodiak Island was substantially smaller in the 1980s than in the 1970s, and the '80s animals were anemic. Researchers concluded the sea lions were suffering nutritional stress.

As mating season approaches each year, male Steller sea

lions head to the rookeries on rocky islands. They arrive in May to stake out and defend a territory. They won't eat for the next 60 days. Six or seven times a day, each breeding male will get face to face with one of the other males and they will hiss at each other, fence with their necks, and even bite. Occasionally, threats escalate into serious fights between animals that have a head roughly the size of a brown/grizzly bear.

Females arrive at the rookeries in late June, give birth, and then mate within 10 days. Females are gregarious during the breeding season. Early observers saw females huddled together and assumed it was a harem devoted to one male. But the females tend to ignore territorial boundaries and dueling males, and they don't hesitate to cross borders while the males are preoccupied with each other. A male will try to herd females back into his territory, often without success. A female commonly gives birth in one territory, mates in another, and moves through many more with her pup.

Two weeks after they're born, pups are swimming in tide pools. Within a month, a pup will accompany its mother on short trips offshore. A nursing female will bite and toss any pup but hers, which she treats to almost 2 quarts of milk per day.

DID YOU KNOW?

STELLER SEA LION: It was named for naturalist Georg Wilhelm Steller, who observed the animals in 1741 and described their lionlike roar, shaggy mane, and long whiskers.

- ◆ **SIZE AND COLOR:** Males 9 feet and 1,500 pounds; females 7 feet and 600 pounds. Light brown.
- ◆ **REPRODUCTION:** Mate in July. Single pup born after 1-year gestation. At birth, 3 feet and 45 pounds.
- ◆ **LIFE SPAN:** Males 20 years, females 30.

- ◆ **FOOD:** Pollock, cod, salmon, herring; occasionally seals, sea otters.
- ◆ **PREDATORS:** Transient killer whales, sharks, humans.
- ◆ **HABITAT AND RANGE:** Coastal areas, especially isolated islands. Southeast Alaska, Gulf of Alaska, Aleutian Islands, Bering Sea.

WALRUS

A female walrus can sleep at sea by inflating her lungs like balloons. Male walrus have an air sac on each side of their neck that they can inflate to the size of basketballs. The male's air sacs serve another purpose: they act as resonating chambers to add depth and volume to his love song.

During mating season, several males will station themselves near a group of females, but only the dominant male sings. The singing is done underwater. The male begins his song with a ringing sound that's often compared to church bells. He follows with an intricate series of knocks and taps, and finishes about 7 minutes later with a flourish of bells. A male will repeat this sequence over and over for hours. Walrus singing goes on all year long, but it peaks during mating season.

When walrus drop into the sea from boulders or cliffs, they land on their side or back to prevent damage to their tusks. Those tusks are actually elongated canine teeth and grow on both males and females. They can grow to a length of 39 inches and weigh up to 12 pounds. Walrus hook their tusks on ice floes to help pull themselves out of the water; in fact, their Latin name, *Odobenus rosmarus*, means "tooth walker." Alaska Fish and Game biologist John Burns saw a walrus "demolish a piece of ice to free her calf, which had fallen into a crevasse. The tusks were as effective as a pick-ax."

Walrus don't use their tusks for digging food from the ocean floor. Instead, they dive as deep as 200 feet and root around in the sea bottom with their broad muzzle. Walrus have about 400 stiff, sensitive bristles on their muzzle with which they can distinguish objects as small as a marble. Once they locate clams or other invertebrates, walrus mouth them and use suction to extract the choicest parts. A walrus consumes 5 to 7 percent of its body weight in food each day—a couple of hundred pounds of food for a good-size male.

During prolonged dives, the flow of blood to the walrus's skin and extremities becomes restricted to maintain a higher body-core temperature. When the walrus hauls out of the water, its blood-starved skin is a pale off-white. Then blood vessels on the skin dilate, and the walrus gradually changes color from white to an off-pink to its normal rust-brown. On crowded walrus beaches, you can see a few pink walrus shading their eyes with a flipper; they look like they're suffering from sunburn.

DID YOU KNOW?

WALRUS:
Rogue walrus have been known to kill polar bears, belugas, and seals by grasping them with their front flippers and stabbing them with their tusks.

◆ **SIZE AND COLOR:** Males 10 feet and 4,000 pounds; females 8½ feet and 2,000 pounds. White in water; pink after emerging from water, then reddish brown.

◆ **REPRODUCTION:** Mate from February to March. Single calf born in April or May. At birth, 4 feet and 150 pounds.

◆ **LIFE SPAN:** 30 to 35 years.

◆ **FOOD:** Clams and mussels; also snails, crabs, shrimp, worms, seals.

◆ **PREDATORS:** Transient killer whales, polar bears, humans.

◆ **HABITAT AND RANGE:** Shallow water close to land. On the Bering Sea ice pack in winter. In summer, females and immature walrus follow the pack ice north into the Chukchi Sea. Males summer at Round Island in Bristol Bay or on Russian islands near Bering Strait.

Humpback whale breaches off the north end of Chichagof Island, Southeast Alaska.

Where to View Alaska's Mammals

I've taken friends from the Lower 48 to look for moose in Kenai National Wildlife Refuge and been skunked—only to return to Anchorage and discover a moose standing in my driveway. Finding Alaska's mammals can be like that. Even in a place as rich in wildlife as Denali National Park and Preserve, there's no guarantee you'll see the animals you're looking for. But there are certain spots where people are usually successful. In the listings that follow, I've noted sites where you might see the mammals featured in this book. The locations are grouped according to the state's six biogeographic regions (see the map on page 87), from south to north.

The focus is on places that are accessible by car, boat, or aircraft or by a short walk. You can see a lot of wildlife from Alaska's roads, which are well marked with numbered mileposts. But many places are accessible only by water or by air. Bush planes or helicopters provide quick access to remote areas. Boats ranging in size from cruise ships to sea kayaks will take you into Alaska's marine world. Rafting companies offer float trips on many of Alaska's rivers. Whether you plan to walk, drive, fly, or boat, you can arrange tours and transportation from almost any town in Alaska. Contact the local chamber of commerce or visitor center for information.

It really pays to ask local residents about wildlife. In Skagway, for example, residents know that you can watch harbor seals from the docks and that the best time to see the seals is when they feed on spawning salmon in August. Locals may also tell you to keep your eyes open for sea otters; a family of five frequented the ore terminal dock during the summer of 1994.

As you experience opportunities to get close to Alaska's mammals, keep in mind that they are rarely as happy to see us as we are to see them. They're not comfortable if we get too close or approach too quickly. You're probably too close if you see any of these signs of stress in an animal: raising its head and cocking its ears toward you; jumping at sound or movement; raising its hackles; lowering its head and flattening its ears. Keep your distance from defensive mothers with young, especially bears and moose. Binoculars and telephoto camera lenses let you get a close look without disturbing the wildlife.

SOUTHEAST ALASKA

Alaska Marine Highway: The state-operated ferries that connect communities throughout Southeast and Southcentral Alaska provide good opportunities to see both land and marine mammals. On-board naturalists point out the best viewing areas.

Glacier Bay National Park and Preserve: Brown/grizzly bears are most often seen in the upper reaches of the west arm of Glacier Bay. Throughout the rest of the park, black bears feed along the beaches during May and June. Humpback and killer whales are widely distributed in Glacier Bay and are best seen in July, while Steller sea lions haul out on the Marble Islands in September. In May and June, harbor seals give birth to their pups on ice floes near tidewater glaciers at the upper reaches of the west arm and Johns Hopkins Inlet. Watch for mountain goats near Mount Wright. Porcupines waddle along walking trails near Glacier Bay Lodge/Park Headquarters.

Gustavus: This area just outside Glacier Bay National Park and Preserve, including Point Adolphus and Icy Strait, may be the best location in Alaska for summer viewing of humpback whales. Charter boats from Gustavus take people whale-watching. Flightseeing trips are available from Gustavus.

Skagway: From boats, you can see Dall porpoises and occasional humpback whales in Long Bay or at Dyea. People see mountain goats from the Klondike Highway north of town. Black bears are also seen along the highway, especially early in spring. There are arctic ground squirrels in town.

Haines: Rafters on the Chilkat and Klehini rivers occasionally spot moose and brown/grizzly bears. Humpback whales (in the summer), killer whales, Dall porpoises, Steller sea lions, harbor seals, and moose can be seen if you beachcomb along the Coastline Trail in Chilkat State Park, 7 miles southeast of Haines.

Juneau: Kayakers and boaters may see deer and Steller sea lions in a string of islands northwest of Juneau in the Lynn Canal. Try Auke Bay and the south end of Douglas Island in May and June for humpback whales and killer whales. There are distant mountain goats on the slopes above Mendenhall Glacier, 13 miles by road northwest of downtown Juneau. Flightseeing is popular in Juneau. The Pack Creek Brown Bear Sanctuary on Admiralty Island attracts lots of bears and people. There is limited entry for humans; visitors must first obtain a permit from the office of the Tongass National Forest, in Juneau.

SIBERIA

CHUKCHI
SEA

ARCTIC
OCEAN

G SEA

ARCTIC

•Barrow

•Kotzebue

Nome

Prudhoe
Bay

vak
nd

Arctic National
Wildlife Refuge

Yukon River

ALASKA

Yukon

ARCTIC CIRCLE

River

WESTERN

INTERIOR

•Fairbanks

•Dillingham

Denali Nat'l
Park & Preserve

STOL
AY

Peninsula

USA
CANADA

aska

Mt. Katmai

•Anchorage

UTHWESTERN

SOUTHCENTRAL

YUKON
TERRITORY

•Cordova

Kodiak Island

Prince William
Sound

GULF OF
ALASKA

Glacier Bay National
Park & Preserve

BRITISH
COLUMBIA

•Juneau

Sitka •

SOUTHEAST

•Wrangell

PACIFIC OCEAN

Alaska's Biogeographic Regions

ee current official road maps for details of particular regions.

0 miles 100

0 km 100

Access is by floatplane or charter boat. From boats in Tracy Arm, watch for killer whales and for harbor seals with pups on icebergs. Scan the slopes for mountain goats, brown/grizzly bears, black bears, and occasional wolverines. From July through September, humpbacks and killer whales are in lower Stephens Passage, about halfway between Juneau and Petersburg.

Sitka: On charter boat trips, people often see harbor seals, sea otters, brown bears, and Sitka black-tailed deer. A few humpback whales stay in the area year-round, though most are seen in summer. In spring, watch for migrating gray whales from Miller Point, Narrow Cape, or Spruce Cape.

Petersburg: Wrangell Narrows, a segment of the Inside Passage just south of town, is a good spot to watch for sea otters, Dall porpoises, harbor seals, Steller sea lions, porcupines, black bears, and Sitka black-tailed deer. You can look for these by boat or from the waterside road.

Wrangell: In July and August when salmon are spawning, Anan Creek in the Tongass National Forest may offer the best black bear viewing in Alaska. It's 30 miles from town by air or charter boat. For access information, contact the U.S. Forest Service in Juneau.

Misty Fiords National Monument: You can reach this area by boat or air charter from Ketchikan. Black bears and river otters can be seen along the coastal wetlands and beaches. Mountain goats and Sitka black-tailed deer are found in alpine areas during the summer. Marine mammals include Dall porpoises, harbor seals, killer whales, and humpback whales.

SOUTHCENTRAL ALASKA

Hatcher Pass/Independence Mine State Historical Park: This area north of Wasilla and Palmer is a great place for arctic ground squirrels, and you might spot pikas and hoary marmots.

Anchorage: From the waterfront, people sometimes see beluga whales at the mouth of Ship Creek. Try for moose at the Eagle River visitor center in nearby Chugach State Park, especially in autumn. In June, scan the slopes above the visitor center for Dall sheep with lambs. At Eklutna Lake, also in the park, look for Dall sheep on the mountainsides. Dall sheep and beluga whales are often seen beside the Seward Highway at Beluga Point, about 16 miles south of Anchorage.

Portage Glacier: During the winter, moose are common in

Portage Valley, a 50-mile drive southeast of Anchorage. In summer, you can see mountain goats on rocky cliffs above timberline during a tour boat ride to the glacier.

Kenai: As the tide comes in on the Kenai River, watch for beluga whales from the end of Bluff Street, right in town. Although belugas can be seen in summer and fall, the best time is April and May. Winter visitors might catch a glimpse of the secretive lynx along Swanson River and Skilak Lake roads. In the Kenai National Wildlife Refuge, watch for moose and black bears along Swanson Lake Road, Swan Lake Road, and Skilak Lake Road.

Homer/Seldovia: From boats and aircraft, people see humpback whales, killer whales, sea otters, Steller sea lions, and Dall porpoises, plus red foxes and black bears on the shoreline. In the Barren Islands southwest of the Kenai Peninsula, humpback and killer whales are seen in mid-June and July.

Seward: Harbor seals and sea otters can be spotted on the waterfront. Seward is the gateway to Kenai Fjords National Park and Preserve. From charter boats, people see humpback whales, killer whales, Dall porpoises, Steller sea lions, sea otters, mountain goats, and black bears. Gray whales migrate through the area in April.

Prince William Sound: This area harbors humpback whales, killer whales, Dall porpoises, Steller sea lions, sea otters, mountain goats, Sitka black-tailed deer, brown/grizzly bears, and black bears. From the communities of Cordova, Valdez, and Whittier, you can visit the sound by boat or aircraft.

Cordova: From the Copper River Highway, look for moose, weasels, river otters, snowshoe hares, and black bears. The Copper River Delta is home to the highest concentration of beavers in the world. Between mileposts 41 and 45, watch for mountain goats. Look for moose at mileposts 19.5 and 22.9 and brown/grizzly bears at milepost 11.5. Sea otters are often spotted from the road going west out of town.

INTERIOR ALASKA

Steese Highway: Arctic ground squirrels are common along this highway that runs northeast from Fairbanks. Caribou are seen between Twelvemile Summit (milepost 85) and Eagle Summit (milepost 107).

Fairbanks: One of the best places in Alaska to look for

cow moose with calves is along Chena Hot Springs Road in Chena River State Recreation Area, east of Fairbanks (milepost 32.8 and milepost 41.5). Arctic ground squirrels are common, and beavers are frequently seen at dusk in the Chena River and its sloughs. To find moose, red foxes, and snowshoe hares, try taking a short walk in the Creamer's Field Migratory Waterfowl Refuge at dawn or dusk.

Denali National Park and Preserve: Denali is the place in Alaska where people often see the big four—brown/grizzly bears, moose, caribou, and Dall sheep. Denali is also the most likely place to see wolves. There are hordes of arctic ground squirrels, pikas near the high passes and around the Eielson visitor center, hoary marmots at Polychrome Pass, wolverines, and red foxes. Shuttle and tour buses transport visitors the length of the 90-mile park road. Look for beavers at Horseshoe Lake near the visitor center. In May, watch for Dall sheep on the mountains above the Savage River and brown/grizzly bears along the river. Caribou and moose are seen along the first 12 miles of road in September.

Denali Highway: Look for caribou, brown/grizzly bears, and moose at milepost 13 and milepost 21.5 (Tangle Lakes); red foxes and wolves also have been seen at milepost 13. In September, listen and look for pikas near Tangle Lakes. There are caribou, brown/grizzly bears, moose, and beavers at Fiftymile Lake at milepost 50.

SOUTHWEST ALASKA

McNeil River State Game Sanctuary: People fly in from Homer to view the greatest concentration of brown/grizzly bears in the world when they feed on salmon here in late summer. Contact the Alaska Department of Fish and Game for details on how to apply for one of the few visiting permits.

Katmai National Park and Preserve: The park is one of the best brown bear viewing areas in Alaska. Dozens of brown/grizzly bears arrive at Brooks Falls from mid-July through September to feed on spawning red salmon. Access is via floatplane to Brooks Camp. A permit is required for the campground; the U.S. National Park Service has current information on permits.

Kodiak Island: Kodiak bears (a subspecies of brown/grizzly bear) can be best seen from boats or planes. Red foxes and Sitka black-tailed deer can be seen from the road. Look for Steller sea lions at the boat docks. Boats provide access to marine waters that are home to harbor seals, sea otters, and Steller sea lions, plus humpback, gray, and killer whales.

Pribilof Islands: The Pribilofs are the place to view fur seals in July and August. Eighty percent of the world's population of northern fur seals hauls out here during the mating season. Access is by plane to St. Paul and St. George islands.

WESTERN ALASKA

Nome/Seward Peninsula: There are about 240 miles of gravel road in the Nome area. To see brown/grizzly bears, red foxes, moose, hoary marmots, and wolves, try Salmon Lake, 40 miles north of Nome on the Nome–Taylor Highway. Musk oxen are occasionally seen from the road system, especially near the Feather River north of Nome. Early in spring, ringed seals and walrus can be spotted from the Nome shoreline. From airplanes, you can spot thousands of migrating caribou in spring and fall.

Nunivak Island: This island is the place to view musk oxen. Photographers visit in late April or early May, when calves are born. Access is via plane from Bethel.

Round Island: Round Island is Alaska's premier place for walrus. Floatplanes and boats from Togiak or Dillingham take people to see bull walrus that haul out on the island for the summer.

ARCTIC ALASKA

Arctic National Wildlife Refuge: The refuge is home to brown/grizzly bears, caribou, arctic foxes, wolves, musk oxen, and Dall sheep. You can fly in to the refuge and raft down its rivers.

Barrow: Bowhead whales travel along the edges of shorefast ice in April and May. In late June, beluga whales congregate in Kasegaluk Lagoon, which is accessible by charter aircraft from Barrow or Kotzebue.

Dalton Highway: This gravel highway begins in central Alaska and ends more than 400 miles later on Alaska's North Slope at Prudhoe Bay. Some of the highway is open to private vehicles; for information on access and permits, contact the State Department of Transportation in Fairbanks. Musk oxen are sometimes seen from the highway near Franklin Bluffs. Brown/grizzly bears, caribou, moose, and red foxes may be spotted along the route; Dall sheep can be seen in the mountains. Look for arctic foxes and arctic ground squirrels at Prudhoe Bay.

SUGGESTED READING

Alaska Geographic Society. *Alaska's Bears*. Anchorage: Alaska Geographic Society, 1993.

Chadwick, Douglas. *A Beast the Color of Winter: The Mountain Goat Observed*. San Francisco: Sierra Club Books, 1983.

Chapman, J. A., and G. A. Feldhamer. *Wild Mammals of North America: Biology-Management-Economics*. Baltimore and London: Johns Hopkins University Press, 1982.

D'Vincent, Cynthia. *Voyaging with the Whales*. Toronto: McClelland & Stewart, 1989. (humpback whales)

Haley, Delphine, et al. *Marine Mammals of Eastern North Pacific and Arctic Waters*. 2d ed. Seattle: Pacific Search Press, 1986.

Henry, J. David. *Red Fox: The Catlike Canine*. Washington, D.C.: Smithsonian Institution Press, 1986.

Hodgson, Bryan. "Hard Harvest on the Bering Sea." *National Geographic*, October 1992, 70. (commercial fishing versus wildlife)

Hull, Cheryl, et al. *Wildlife Notebook Series*. Juneau: Alaska Department of Fish and Game, 1994.

Leatherwood, Stephen, and Randall R. Reeves. *Sierra Club Handbook of Whales and Dolphins*. San Francisco: Sierra Club Books, 1983.

Leatherwood, Stephen, Randall R. Reeves, and Brent S. Stewart. *Sierra Club Handbook of Seals and Sirenians*. San Francisco: Sierra Club Books, 1992.

Lopez, Barry Holstun. *Of Wolves and Men*. New York: Charles Scribner's Sons, 1978.

Matkin, Craig O. *Guide to the Killer Whales of Prince William Sound*. Valdez, Alaska: Prince William Sound Books, 1994.

Mech, L. David. *The Way of the Wolf*. Stillwater, Minn.: Voyageur Press, 1991.

Murie, Adolph. *The Wolves of Mount McKinley*. Washington, D.C.: U.S. Government Printing Office, 1944.

Murray, John A., ed. *The Great Bear: Contemporary Writings on the Grizzly*. Seattle: Alaska Northwest Books, 1992.

———. *Out Among the Wolves: Contemporary Writings on the Wolf*. Seattle: Alaska Northwest Books, 1993.

National Geographic Society. *Wild Animals of North America*. Washington, D.C.: National Geographic Society, 1979.

Obee, Bruce, and Graeme Ellis. *Guardians of the Whales: The Quest to Study Whales in the Wild*. Seattle: Alaska Northwest Books, 1992.

Oceanic Society Staff. *Field Guide to the Gray Whale*. Seattle: Sasquatch Books, 1989.

O'Clair, Rita M., Robert H. Armstrong, and Richard Carstensen. *The Nature of Southeast Alaska: A Guide to Plants, Animals, and Habitats*. Seattle: Alaska Northwest Books, 1992.

Orr, Robert T. *The Little Known Pika*. New York: Macmillan, 1977.

Paine, Stefani. *The World of the Sea Otter*. San Francisco: Sierra Club Books, 1993.

Peacock, Doug. *Grizzly Years: In Search of the American Wilderness*. New York: Henry Holt, 1990.

Riedman, Marianne. *The Pinnipeds: Seals, Sea Lions, and Walruses*. Berkeley: University of California Press, 1990.

Rose, Uldis. *The North American Porcupine*. Washington, D.C.: Smithsonian Institution Press, 1989.

Runtz, Michael W. P. *Moose Country: Saga of the Woodland Moose*. Minoqua, Wis.: NorthWord Press, 1991.

Stall, Chris. *Animal Tracks of Alaska*. Seattle: The Mountaineers, 1993.

Walker, Tom. *Denali Journal*. Harrisburg, Pa.: Stackpole Books, 1992.

———. *River of Bears*. Stillwater, Minn.: Voyageur Press, 1993.

Wynne, Kate. *Marine Mammals of Alaska*. Fairbanks: Alaska Sea Grant College Program, 1992.

INDEX

Admiralty Island, 86
Alaska Marine Highway, 86
Alaska Peninsula, 20
Aleutian Islands, 78, 80
Amchitka Island, 78
Anan Creek, 88
Anchorage, 88
Arctic Alaska, 91
arctic fox, 12–13, 43, 77, 91
arctic ground squirrel, 14–15, 86, 89–91
Arctic National Wildlife Refuge, 8, 75, 91
Auke Bay, 86

baleen, 60–61, 64, 69
Banks Island, 60
Barren Islands, 89
Barrow, 91
bear
    black, 18–19, 21, 86, 88–89
    brown/grizzly, 14–15, 19, 20–21, 26, 74, 86, 88–91
    Kodiak, 90. See also brown/grizzly bear
    polar, 7–8, 13, 74–75, 77
beaver, 16–17, 89–90
Beluga Point, 88
beluga whale, 58–59, 88–89, 91
Bering Sea, 59–61, 64
Bering Strait, 60
black bear, 18–19, 21, 86, 88–89
black-tailed deer, Sitka, 48–49, 88–90
bowhead whale, 60–61, 91
Brooks Falls, 90
brown/grizzly bear, 14–15, 19, 20–21, 26, 74, 86, 88–91. See also Kodiak bear
bubble net, 69

caribou, 8, 22–23, 89–91
Chena Hot Springs Road, 90
Chena River State Recreation Area, 90
Chilkat River, 86
Chilkat State Park, 86
Chugach State Park, 8, 88

Chukchi Sea, 64–65
Copper River Delta, 89
Copper River Highway, 89
Cordova, 89
Creamer's Field Migratory Waterfowl Refuge, 90

Dall porpoise, 62–63, 86, 88–89
Dall sheep, 8, 24–25, 29, 34, 88, 90–91
Dalton Highway, 91
deer, Sitka black-tailed, 48–49, 88–90
Denali Highway, 90
Denali National Park and Preserve, 22, 90
Douglas Island, 86
Dyea, 86

Eagle River visitor center, 88
Eielson visitor center, 90
Eklutna Lake, 8, 88
ermine, 47. See also short-tailed weasel

Fairbanks, 89–90
Feather River, 91
Fiftymile Lake, 90
Fort Yukon, 58
fox
    arctic, 12–13, 43, 77, 91
    red, 42–43, 89–91
Franklin Bluffs, 91

Glacier Bay National Park and Preserve, 86
goat, mountain, 34–35, 86, 88–89
gray whale, 8–9, 64–65, 88, 91
grizzly bear. See brown/grizzly bear
Gulf of Alaska, 80
Gustavus, 86

Haines, 86
harbor porpoise, 62–63
harbor seal, 66–67, 85–86, 88, 89
hare, snowshoe, 28–29, 50–51, 89–90

Hatcher Pass/ Independence Mine State Historical Park, 88
hibernation
    arctic ground squirrel, 14
    black bear, 18
    brown/grizzly bear, 20
hoary marmot, 26–27, 88, 90–91
Homer/Seldovia, 89
Horseshoe Lake, 90
humpback whale, 68–69, 86, 88–89, 91

Icy Strait, 86
Interior Alaska, 89–90

Johns Hopkins Inlet, 86
Juneau, 86–88

Kasegaluk Lagoon, 91
Katmai National Park and Preserve, 90
Kenai, 89
Kenai Fjords National Park, 9
Kenai National Wildlife Refuge, 89
Kenai Peninsula, 80
Kenai River, 89
killer whale, 70–71, 86, 88–89, 91
Kleheni River, 86
Klondike Highway, 86
Kodiak bear, 90. See also brown/grizzly bear
Kodiak Island, 20, 48, 80, 90–91

Long Bay, 86
lynx, 28–29, 51, 89

Marble Islands, 86
marmot, hoary, 26–27, 88, 90–91
marten, 30–31
McNeil River State Game Sanctuary, 90
Mendenhall Glacier, 86
migration
    caribou, 22–23
    gray whale, 64–65
    humpback whale, 68
Miller Point, 88

Misty Fiords National Monument, 88
moose, 32–33, 86, 89–91
Mount Wright, 86
mountain goat, 34–35, 86, 88–89
musk ox, 36–37, 91

Narrow Cape, 88
Nome/Seward Peninsula, 91
northern fur seal, 8, 72–73, 91
Nunivak Island, 36, 91

otter
   river, 44–45, 88–89
   sea, 78–79, 85, 88–89
ox, musk, 36–37, 91

Pack Creek Brown Bear Sanctuary, 86
Petersburg, 88
pika, 38–39, 88, 90
Point Adolphus, 86
Point Barrow, 75
polar bear, 7–8, 13, 74–75, 77
Polychrome Pass, 90
porcupine, 40–41, 86, 88
porpoise
   Dall, 62–63, 86, 88–89
   harbor, 62–63
Portage Glacier, 88–89
Pribilof Islands, 8, 73, 91
Prince William Sound, 48, 78, 89
Prudhoe Bay, 91

qiviut, 36

red fox, 42–43, 89–91
red squirrel, 50
ringed seal, 76–77, 91
river otter, 44–45, 88–89
Round Island, 8, 91

Salmon Lake, 91
Savage River, 90
sea lion, Steller, 9, 80–81, 86, 89–91
sea otter, 78–79, 85, 88–89
seal
   harbor, 66–67, 85–86, 88, 89
   northern fur, 8, 72–73, 91
   ringed, 76–77, 91
Seward, 89
Seward Highway, 88
Seward Peninsula, 20
sheep, Dall, 8, 24–25, 29, 34, 88, 90–91
Ship Creek, 88
short-tailed weasel, 46–47
Sitka, 88
Sitka black-tailed deer, 48–49, 88–90
Skagway, 85–86
Skilak Lake Road, 89
snowshoe hare, 28–29, 50–51, 89–90
Southcentral Alaska, 88–89
Southeast Alaska, 86–88
Southwest Alaska, 90–91
Spruce Cape, 88

squirrel, arctic ground, 14–15, 86, 89–91
Steese Highway, 89
Steller, Georg Wilhelm, 81
Steller sea lion, 9, 80–81, 86, 89–91
Stephens Passage, 88
Swan Lake Road, 89
Swanson Lake Road, 89
Swanson River Road, 89

Tangle Lakes, 90
Tongass National Forest, 88
Tracy Arm, 86

Valdez, 89

walrus, 8, 82–83, 91
weasel, short-tailed, 46–47, 89
Western Alaska, 91
whale
   beluga, 58–59, 88–89, 91
   bowhead, 60–61, 91
   gray, 8–9, 64–65, 88, 91
   humpback, 68–69, 86, 88–89, 91
   killer, 70–71, 86, 88–89, 91
Whittier, 89
wolf, 52–53, 90–91
wolverine, 54–55, 88, 90
Wrangell, 88
Wrangell Narrows, 88

Alaska Northwest Books™ is proud to publish another book in its Alaska Pocket Guide series, designed with the curious traveler in mind. Ask for more books in this series at your favorite bookstore, or contact Alaska Northwest Books™.

ALASKA NORTHWEST BOOKS™

An Imprint of Graphic Arts Center Publishing Company
P.O. Box 10306, Portland, OR 97210
800-452-3032